Kotlin Android Development

A Beginner's guide to creating modern mobile app

By Arthur Richard

Table of Contents

Introduction

Chapter 1: Getting Started with Kotlin

Chapter 2: Android Development Fundamentals

Chapter 3: Building Modern UI with Jetpack Compose

3.1 Introduction to Jetpack Compose

3.2 Creating UI Components in Compose

3.3 Managing State in Compose Applications

3.4 Theming and Styling Your App

3.5 Animations and Transitions in Compose

Chapter 4: Data Management and Networking

4.1 Working with SharedPreferences and Room Database

4.2 Fetching Data from APIs Using Retrofit

4.3 Using Kotlin Flow and LiveData for Data Streams

4.4 Dependency Injection with Hilt

Chapter 5: Advanced Android Concepts

5.1 Background Tasks with WorkManager and Coroutines

5.2 Integrating Firebase (Authentication, Firestore)

5.3 Handling Permissions and Security Best Practices

5.4 Performance Optimization and Debugging

Chapter 6: Testing and Deployment

Chapter 7: Building a Complete App – A Hands-On Project

Conclusion and Next Steps

- <u>Best Practices for Kotlin Android Developers</u>
- <u>Resources for Further Learning</u>
- <u>Exploring Advanced Topics (Kotlin Multiplatform, AI in Apps)</u>

Introduction

Why Choose Kotlin for Android Development?

Imagine building an Android app with clean, concise, and modern code—without the verbosity and boilerplate of Java. That's what Kotlin brings to the table. If you've ever felt frustrated with unnecessary complexity in your code, Kotlin is here to make your life easier.

Kotlin is an expressive, safe, and modern programming language that is now the official preferred language for Android development. In 2017, Google announced support for Kotlin, and by 2019, they went even further—declaring Kotlin as the primary language for Android development. That's a big deal! Today, most professional Android developers have already switched to Kotlin, and new apps are being built with it from the ground up.

So, what makes Kotlin special?

Concise – Say goodbye to excessive boilerplate code. Kotlin allows you to achieve more with fewer lines.

Safe – No more NullPointerException headaches! Kotlin has built-in null safety to help you avoid crashes.

Interoperable – Already have a Java-based project? No worries! Kotlin works seamlessly with existing Java code.

Modern & Expressive – Features like coroutines, extension functions, and smart casts make Kotlin a joy to work with.

If you want to future-proof your Android development skills and build apps faster, Kotlin is the way forward.

Who This Book is For

Are you a complete beginner to Android development? Or maybe you've dabbled in Java and want to switch to Kotlin? Either way, this book is for you.

This book is **beginner-friendly** and assumes no prior experience in Kotlin or Android development. We'll start from the absolute basics and gradually build up to more advanced topics. By the time you finish, you'll have built a real-world app and gained the confidence to explore Android development further.

This book is perfect for:

1. Aspiring app developers who want to learn Kotlin and Android from scratch.
2. Java developers looking to transition to Kotlin for modern Android development.
3. Students, hobbyists, or professionals who want to build Android apps with up-to-date best practices.

Tools and Setup

Before we start coding, let's get our development environment ready. You'll need a few essential tools:

1. Android Studio (The Official IDE)

Android Studio is Google's official development environment for Android apps. It comes with everything you need, including an emulator, a code editor, and debugging tools.

Download & Install:

1. Go to developer.android.com/studio.
2. Download the latest version for your operating system (Windows, macOS, or Linux).
3. Install it by following the on-screen instructions.

Once installed, launch Android Studio. The first time you open it, it will guide you through a setup wizard to install necessary components like the Android SDK and emulator.

2. JDK (Java Development Kit)

Even though we'll be using Kotlin, Android still requires the Java Development Kit (JDK) to run. The good news? Android Studio includes OpenJDK by default, so you don't need to install it separately.

3. Android Emulator or Real Device

You have two options for testing your apps:

- **Android Emulator** – Comes built into Android Studio. Great for quick testing, but can be slow.
- **Real Device** – If you have an Android phone, you can enable **Developer Mode** and **USB Debugging** to test apps directly.

To set up your Android phone for development:

1. Go to **Settings > About Phone** and tap **Build Number** seven times.
2. Go back to **Developer Options** and enable **USB Debugging**.
3. Connect your phone to your computer via USB, and you're ready to go.

Overview of Modern Android Development Trends

The Android ecosystem is constantly evolving, and staying updated with the latest best practices will make you a more efficient developer. Here are some key trends shaping modern Android development:

1. Jetpack Compose – The Future of UI Design

Forget XML layouts—Jetpack Compose is the new way to build UIs in Android. It allows you to design interfaces using Kotlin code, making UI development more intuitive and flexible. We'll cover Jetpack Compose in detail later in the book.

2. Kotlin Coroutines – Simplified Asynchronous Programming

Handling background tasks like API calls and database operations can be tricky. Coroutines make it easier to write async code that's both readable and efficient.

3. Modularization – Better Code Organization

Modern Android projects are breaking their code into modules to improve maintainability, speed up builds, and enable team collaboration.

4. Dependency Injection with Hilt

Managing dependencies in large apps can be a nightmare. Hilt, a modern DI library, makes this process seamless and helps keep your code clean.

5. Kotlin Multiplatform – Cross-Platform Development

Want to share code between Android and iOS? Kotlin Multiplatform is gaining popularity as a solution for writing shared business logic across platforms.

Now that we've set the stage, it's time to start coding! In the next chapter, we'll take our first steps with Kotlin, covering everything from variables and functions to object-oriented programming. By the end, you'll be comfortable writing Kotlin code and ready to start building Android apps.

Chapter 1: Getting Started with Kotlin

Welcome to your first step into Kotlin programming! Before we dive into Android app development, it's essential to get comfortable with Kotlin—the language that will power your apps. Think of this chapter as your foundation. Master these basics, and the rest of your journey will feel much smoother.

1.1 Setting Up Your Development Environment

Before we dive into Kotlin and Android development, let's get your workspace ready. A **well-configured development environment** is crucial for a smooth coding experience.

Choosing the Right Tools

For **Kotlin Android development**, you'll primarily need:

1. **Android Studio** – The official IDE for Android development
2. **Java Development Kit (JDK)** – Required for running Kotlin and Gradle
3. **Android SDK & Emulator** – Tools for testing apps
4. **A Physical Android Device (Optional)** – For real-world testing

Let's get everything installed and configured.

Installing Android Studio

Android Studio is an all-in-one IDE that includes the **Android SDK, an emulator, and build tools**. Google actively maintains it, ensuring compatibility with the latest Android versions.

Step 1: Download & Install

1. Go to the official site: Android Studio Download
2. Download the latest stable version for **Windows, macOS, or Linux**.
3. Run the installer and follow the setup wizard.

During installation, choose:
  Standard installation – Comes with recommended settings
  Android SDK & Emulator – Select default options

Tip: Ensure you have at least **8GB of RAM and 10GB of free disk space** for smooth performance.

Configuring Android Studio

Once installed, open Android Studio and:

1. Set Up the Android SDK

- Open **Preferences (Settings on Windows)** → **Appearance & Behavior** → **System Settings** → **Android SDK**.
- Ensure the latest **SDK version** and necessary tools (like build-tools, platform-tools) are installed.

Why is this important? The SDK contains APIs and system images required to build and test Android apps.

2. Install a Virtual Device (Emulator)

While real devices are great for testing, an **Android emulator** is essential for debugging.

How to Set Up an Emulator:

1. Open **Android Studio > Device Manager**
2. Click **Create Virtual Device**
3. Choose a popular device (e.g., Pixel 6)
4. Download and select a **System Image (Recommended: API Level 34+)**
5. Click **Finish**, then **Launch the Emulator**

Tip: Enable **hardware acceleration (HAXM for Intel, Hyper-V for AMD)** to improve emulator speed.

Setting Up Kotlin in Android Studio

Kotlin is the default language for Android development, and Android Studio has **built-in support**.

Creating Your First Kotlin Project

1. Open Android Studio and click **New Project**.
2. Select **Empty Activity** (or Jetpack Compose if you prefer modern UI development).
3. Set **Language** to **Kotlin**.
4. Click **Finish**—your first Kotlin project is ready!

Why Kotlin? It's **concise, safer, and more modern** compared to Java, making Android development **faster and more efficient**.

Gradle Configuration for Kotlin

Gradle is Android's **build automation tool**, handling dependencies, compilation, and APK generation.

Checking Your Gradle Setup

In **build.gradle (Module: app)**, ensure:

```
plugins {

    id 'com.android.application'

    id 'kotlin-android'

}
```

This enables Kotlin support in your project.

Running Your First Kotlin Android App

1. Click **Run (▶)** in Android Studio.
2. Choose **an emulator or a real device**.
3. If successful, you'll see **"Hello World!"** on the screen.

If you face issues, here are some common fixes:

Issue	Solution
Android Studio runs slowly	Enable hardware acceleration & increase RAM allocation
Emulator won't start	Check **AVD settings** and enable virtualization (BIOS)
Gradle sync errors	Update dependencies and re-sync **(File > Sync Project with Gradle Files)**
Kotlin isn't recognized	Ensure **Kotlin plugin** is enabled (Preferences > Plugins > Kotlin)

Keep Android Studio and the SDK updated to avoid compatibility issues.

1.2 Kotlin Basics: Variables, Data Types, and Functions

Kotlin is a **concise, expressive, and type-safe** programming language. Understanding its **core building blocks**—variables, data types, and functions—is essential before diving into Android development.

Variables in Kotlin

A **variable** is a container that holds data. In Kotlin, variables are **statically typed**, meaning their type is determined at compile time.

Two Types of Variables:

1. **Immutable (val)** – Cannot be changed (like final in Java)
2. **Mutable (var)** – Can be reassigned

val name = "Kotlin" // Immutable

var age = 25   // Mutable

Best Practice: Prefer val unless you need to modify the value. This makes code safer and avoids accidental changes.

Data Types in Kotlin

Kotlin has a strong type system, preventing **unexpected errors**. Here are the primary types:

1. Numeric Types

Kotlin provides multiple number types, but in most cases, Int and Double are enough.

val intNumber: Int = 10

val doubleNumber: Double = 3.14

2. Boolean Type

A Boolean stores either true or false.

val isKotlinFun: Boolean = true

3. String and Char

A String represents text, while Char stores a single character.

val greeting: String = "Hello, Kotlin!"

val letter: Char = 'K'

4. Collections: Lists and Maps

Collections store multiple values. Kotlin provides:

Immutable List (listOf) – Cannot be modified

Mutable List (mutableListOf) – Can be updated

Map (mapOf) – Key-value pairs

```kotlin
val fruits = listOf("Apple", "Banana", "Cherry")  // Immutable
```

```kotlin
val scores = mutableMapOf("Alice" to 85, "Bob" to 90)  // Mutable
```

Tip: Use listOf when you don't need to modify a collection, ensuring safety.

Type Inference & Type Conversion

Kotlin can **infer types** automatically:

```kotlin
val language = "Kotlin"  // Inferred as String
```

However, explicit type conversion is needed between different types:

```kotlin
val number = 10
```

```kotlin
val pi = number.toDouble()  // Converts Int to Double
```

Why? Kotlin prevents unintended type mismatches, reducing runtime errors.

Functions in Kotlin

Functions **group reusable logic**, making code cleaner.

Defining a Function

```kotlin
fun greet(name: String): String {

    return "Hello, $name!"

}
```

Tip: Use string templates ($variable) for better readability.

Single-Expression Functions

For simple functions, Kotlin allows a shorter syntax:

```kotlin
fun add(a: Int, b: Int) = a + b
```

Why? This improves readability and reduces boilerplate.

Default & Named Arguments

Kotlin allows **default values** to make function calls flexible:

```kotlin
fun greet(name: String = "Guest") = "Hello, $name!"
```

Now, calling greet() defaults to "Hello, Guest!".

You can also **specify arguments by name**:

```kotlin
fun displayInfo(name: String, age: Int) {

    println("$name is $age years old.")

}
```

```kotlin
displayInfo(age = 30, name = "Alice")  // Named arguments avoid confusion
```

Best Practice: Use **default arguments** to simplify function calls.

Lambda Expressions: Kotlin's Powerful Feature

Lambdas are **concise, anonymous functions** often used for higher-order operations:

```
val square = { num: Int -> num * num }

println(square(4))  // Output: 16
```

Use Case: Lambdas shine in **list transformations, event handling, and functional programming**.

Mastering **variables, data types, and functions** is the first step toward writing clean and efficient Kotlin code. Here are the key takeaways:

Use val for immutability and var for mutability

Kotlin's type system prevents common runtime errors

Functions should be **short, reusable, and expressive**

Lambdas provide **powerful, concise function definitions**

With these fundamentals in place, you're now ready to **explore control flow and object-oriented programming** in Kotlin!

1.3 Control Flow and Loops in Kotlin

Every programming language needs a way to control the **flow of execution**. In Kotlin, this is achieved using:

Conditional Statements (if, when)

Loops (for, while, do-while)

These constructs help your programs make decisions and execute **repetitive tasks efficiently**. By mastering them, you'll write **more dynamic and interactive Kotlin applications**.

1. Conditional Statements: Making Decisions

1.1 if Statement

Kotlin's if works just like in other languages. It checks a condition and executes code accordingly.

```
val temperature = 25

if (temperature > 30) {

    println("It's hot outside!")

} else if (temperature > 20) {

    println("It's a pleasant day.")

} else {

    println("It's quite cold today.")

}
```

Tip: Kotlin allows if expressions to return values.

1.2 if as an Expression

Unlike Java, if in Kotlin **returns a value** and can be used directly in variable assignments.

```kotlin
val age = 18

val status = if (age >= 18) "Adult" else "Minor"


println(status)  // Output: Adult
```

Best Practice: Use this feature to make your code more concise.

1.3 when Statement: A Better Switch Case

The when expression is Kotlin's **powerful replacement for** switch statements. It's cleaner and more flexible.

```kotlin
val day = 3

val dayName = when (day) {

    1 -> "Monday"

    2 -> "Tuesday"

    3 -> "Wednesday"

    4 -> "Thursday"

    5 -> "Friday"

    6, 7 -> "Weekend"

    else -> "Invalid day"

}
```

```kotlin
println(dayName)  // Output: Wednesday
```

Why when? It eliminates **break statements** and allows multiple conditions in one case.

1.4 when with Multiple Conditions

when can handle **multiple types of conditions**—ranges, types, or even function results.

Using Ranges:

```kotlin
val score = 85


val grade = when (score) {

    in 90..100 -> "A"

    in 80..89 -> "B"

    in 70..79 -> "C"

    else -> "F"

}
```

```kotlin
println("Grade: $grade")  // Output: B
```

Using Type Checking:

```kotlin
fun processInput(input: Any) {

    when (input) {

        is String -> println("You entered a string: $input")

        is Int -> println("You entered a number: $input")

        else -> println("Unknown input type")

    }

}

processInput(42)  // Output: You entered a number: 42
```

Best Practice: Use when instead of multiple if-else chains for better readability.

2. Loops: Repeating Tasks Efficiently

Loops are essential for executing code **multiple times** without redundancy. Kotlin provides:

   for loop – Iterates over collections and ranges

while loop – Runs while a condition is true

do-while loop – Runs at least once, then checks the condition

2.1 for Loop: Iterating Over Collections

Looping Through a Range

```
for (i in 1..5) {

    println("Iteration: $i")

}
```

Output:

Iteration: 1

Iteration: 2

Iteration: 3

Iteration: 4

Iteration: 5

Looping Through a List

```
val fruits = listOf("Apple", "Banana", "Cherry")
```

```
for (fruit in fruits) {

    println(fruit)

}
```

Output:

Apple

Banana

Cherry

Looking with Indexes (indices and withIndex())

```
for (index in fruits.indices) {

    println("Index $index: ${fruits[index]}")

}
```

OR

```
for ((index, fruit) in fruits.withIndex()) {

    println("Index $index: $fruit")
```

}

Tip: withIndex() improves readability when working with indexed collections.

2.2 while Loop: Running Until a Condition is Met

A while loop executes **as long as** the condition remains true.

var count = 5

```
while (count > 0) {

    println("Countdown: $count")

    count--

}
```

Output:

Countdown: 5

Countdown: 4

Countdown: 3

Countdown: 2

Countdown: 1

Best Practice: Ensure the condition changes inside the loop, or you'll create an **infinite loop**.

2.3 do-while Loop: Ensuring at Least One Execution

A do-while loop **always runs at least once**, even if the condition is false from the start.

```
var number = 0


do {

    println("Number: $number")

    number++

} while (number < 3)
```

Output:

Number: 0

Number: 1

Number: 2

Use Case: When you need to execute code **at least once**, like user input validation.

3. Loop Control Statements: Controlling Execution

3.1 break: Exiting a Loop Early

```
for (i in 1..5) {

    if (i == 3) break  // Stops at 3

    println(i)

}
```

Output:

```
1

2
```

3.2 continue: Skipping an Iteration

```
for (i in 1..5) {

    if (i == 3) continue  // Skips 3, continues the loop

    println(i)

}
```

Output:

```
1

2
```

4

5

3.3 Labels: Controlling Nested Loops

Labels (@label) help control **nested loops**.

```
outer@ for (i in 1..3) {

    for (j in 1..3) {

        if (i == 2 && j == 2) break@outer  // Exits both loops

        println("i: $i, j: $j")

    }

}
```

Output:

i: 1, j: 1

i: 1, j: 2

i: 1, j: 3

i: 2, j: 1

Best Practice: Use labels sparingly; they can make code harder to read.

Use if for simple conditions and when for multiple cases

Prefer for loops for collections and while loops for condition-based iteration

Leverage loop control (break, continue, labels) for flexibility

Mastering **control flow and loops** makes your Kotlin code **more dynamic and efficient**, paving the way for **object-oriented programming** in the next chapter!

1.4 Object-Oriented Programming in Kotlin

Object-Oriented Programming (OOP) is a **fundamental paradigm** that helps developers organize code in a **modular, reusable, and scalable** way. Kotlin fully supports OOP with **classes, objects, inheritance, interfaces, and more**—but in a more concise and expressive way than Java.

1. Classes and Objects: The Foundation of OOP

A **class** is a blueprint for creating **objects**. An object is an **instance** of a class.

Defining a Class and Creating an Object

```
class Car {

    var brand: String = "Toyota"

    var model: String = "Corolla"



    fun drive() {

        println("The $brand $model is driving.")
```

```
    }

}
```

// Creating an object

```
val myCar = Car()
```

```
myCar.drive()  // Output: The Toyota Corolla is driving.
```

Why use classes? They help organize code by **grouping related properties and functions together**.

2. Constructors: Initializing Objects

Kotlin provides **primary constructors** (directly in the class header) and **secondary constructors** (inside the class body).

Primary Constructor (Recommended)

```
class Car(val brand: String, val model: String) {

    fun drive() {

        println("The $brand $model is driving.")

    }

}
```

```
// Creating an object with parameters

val myCar = Car("Tesla", "Model S")

myCar.drive()  // Output: The Tesla Model S is driving.
```

Best Practice: Use val or var in primary constructors to automatically create properties.

Secondary Constructor (For Special Cases)

```
class Bike {

    var brand: String

    var model: String

    constructor(brand: String, model: String) {

        this.brand = brand

        this.model = model

    }

}
```

Tip: Use secondary constructors **only when additional initialization logic is needed**.

3. Encapsulation: Protecting Data

Encapsulation restricts **direct access to class properties**, allowing control over how they're modified.

Visibility Modifiers in Kotlin:

Modifier	Access Scope
private	Only within the same class
protected	In the same class & subclasses
internal	Inside the same module
public (default)	Anywhere

Encapsulation Example

```kotlin
class BankAccount(private var balance: Double) {

    fun deposit(amount: Double) {

        if (amount > 0) balance += amount
```

```kotlin
    }

    fun getBalance(): Double {

        return balance

    }

}
```

```kotlin
// Creating an object

val account = BankAccount(1000.0)

account.deposit(500.0)

println(account.getBalance())  // Output: 1500.0
```

Best Practice: Use private for sensitive data and provide controlled access via functions.

4. Inheritance: Reusing Code Efficiently

Inheritance allows a class (**child class**) to inherit properties and behaviors from another class (**parent class**).

Defining a Parent and Child Class

```kotlin
// Parent class

open class Animal {
```

```kotlin
    fun eat() {

        println("This animal is eating.")

    }

}


// Child class

class Dog : Animal() {

    fun bark() {

        println("The dog is barking.")

    }

}


// Creating an object

val myDog = Dog()

myDog.eat()  // Output: This animal is eating.

myDog.bark()  // Output: The dog is barking.
```

Note: Use open to make a class **inheritable** (by default, Kotlin classes are final).

Overriding Functions in Subclasses

```kotlin
open class Animal {

    open fun makeSound() {

        println("Animal makes a sound.")

    }

}


class Cat : Animal() {

    override fun makeSound() {

        println("Meow!")

    }

}

val myCat = Cat()

myCat.makeSound()  // Output: Meow!
```

Tip: Always use override when redefining a function from a parent class.

5. Interfaces: Achieving Multiple Inheritance

Since Kotlin doesn't support multiple inheritance, interfaces help achieve abstraction and **code reuse**.

Defining and Implementing an Interface

```kotlin
interface Drivable {

    fun drive()

}

interface Flyable {

    fun fly()

}

class FlyingCar : Drivable, Flyable {

    override fun drive() {

        println("Driving on the road.")

    }


    override fun fly() {

        println("Flying in the sky.")

    }

}

val myFlyingCar = FlyingCar()

myFlyingCar.drive()  // Output: Driving on the road.

myFlyingCar.fly()  // Output: Flying in the sky.
```

Best Practice: Use interfaces to define **common behaviors** without enforcing class hierarchy.

6. Data Classes: Simplifying Data Handling

Kotlin provides **data classes** to **automatically generate** useful functions like toString(), equals(), and copy().

Defining a Data Class

data class User(val name: String, val age: Int)

val user1 = User("Alice", 25)

println(user1) // Output: User(name=Alice, age=25)

Copying Objects

val user2 = user1.copy(age = 26)

println(user2) // Output: User(name=Alice, age=26)

Why use data classes? They reduce boilerplate for **storing and managing data objects**.

 Use classes and objects to structure code efficiently
  Encapsulation ensures data safety and controlled access
  Inheritance promotes code reuse, but favor composition when possible
  Interfaces enable flexible design with multiple behaviors
  Data classes simplify object management

1.5 Introduction to Kotlin Coroutines

Modern apps often need to handle multiple tasks at once—such as downloading data, updating the UI, and responding to user input—all without freezing or slowing down. This is where **asynchronous programming** comes in.

Traditionally, developers used **threads, callbacks, and RxJava** to manage concurrency. But these approaches often led to **complex, hard-to-maintain code**.

Kotlin **coroutines** solve this by providing a **lightweight, readable, and efficient** way to handle concurrency.

1. What Are Coroutines?

A **coroutine** is a **lightweight thread** that allows you to run tasks asynchronously without blocking the main thread.

Unlike traditional threads:

Coroutines are **faster** and consume **less memory**.

They support **structured concurrency**—making them **easier to manage**.

They use **suspend functions** instead of callbacks—leading to **cleaner code**.

Blocking vs. Non-Blocking Code

Consider the **traditional blocking approach**:

```
fun main() {

    Thread.sleep(3000)  // Blocks the main thread for 3 seconds

    println("Task complete")
```

}

Problem: The entire program freezes for 3 seconds.

Now, let's use **coroutines for a non-blocking approach**:

```kotlin
import kotlinx.coroutines.*


fun main() = runBlocking {

    launch {

        delay(3000)  // Suspends without blocking

        println("Task complete")

    }

    println("Hello, world!")

}
```

Output:

Hello, world!

Task complete (After 3 seconds)

 The program **continues running** while waiting for the task to complete!

2. Suspending Functions: The Key to Coroutines

A **suspend function** is a special function that can be **paused and resumed** without blocking the thread.

Defining a Suspend Function

suspend fun fetchData() {

   delay(2000) // Simulates a network request

   println("Data fetched")

}

Important:

  delay(2000) **pauses the function** without blocking the thread.

  Only other **coroutines or suspend functions** can call fetchData().

Calling a Suspend Function

fun main() = runBlocking {

   fetchData()

   println("Processing complete")

}

Output:

(Data fetched after 2 seconds)

Processing complete

  The program **waits** for fetchData() to complete before proceeding.

3. Coroutine Builders: Creating Coroutines

Kotlin provides **three main coroutine builders** to launch coroutines:

Builder	Description	Use Case
launch	Fire-and-forget coroutine	Background tasks
async	Returns a result (Deferred)	When you need a return value
runBlocking	Blocks the main thread	Only for testing or starting coroutines

---

3.1 launch: Fire-and-Forget

```
fun main() = runBlocking {

    launch {

        delay(2000)

        println("Task complete")

    }

    println("Main continues running...")
```

}

launch runs in **parallel** without waiting for the coroutine to finish.

3.2 async: Getting a Result

Unlike launch, async **returns a result** using Deferred.

```
fun main() = runBlocking {

    val result = async {

        delay(2000)

        "Data loaded"

    }

    println("Processing...")

    println(result.await())  // Waits for result

}
```

Output:

Processing...

(Data loaded after 2 seconds)

await() waits for the coroutine to complete **before proceeding**.

4. Coroutine Scopes: Managing Lifecycles

CoroutineScope defines **when a coroutine starts and when it should be canceled**.

Common Scopes in Kotlin

Scope	Description	Use Case
GlobalScope	Runs for the lifetime of the application	Background tasks
runBlocking	Blocks the thread until execution completes	Testing
CoroutineScope	Used in classes to manage coroutines	ViewModel, Repositories

4.1 Using CoroutineScope in a Class

```
class DataManager {

    private val scope = CoroutineScope(Dispatchers.IO)

    fun fetchData() {

        scope.launch {

            delay(2000)
```

```
        println("Data fetched")

    }

  }

}
```

Ensures coroutines are **tied to the class lifecycle**.

5. Dispatchers: Choosing the Right Thread

Coroutines use **dispatchers** to decide **which thread they should run on**.

Dispatcher	Description	Use Case
Dispatchers.Main	Runs on the main (UI) thread	UI updates
Dispatchers.IO	Optimized for background I/O (network, database)	API calls, file handling
Dispatchers.Default	For CPU-intensive tasks	Heavy computations

Dispatchers.Unconfined   Inherits the caller thread   Testing

Example: Switching Dispatchers

```
fun main() = runBlocking {

    launch(Dispatchers.IO) {  // Runs on background thread

        val data = fetchData()

        withContext(Dispatchers.Main) {  // Switches to UI thread

            println("Updating UI with: $data")

        }

    }

}

suspend fun fetchData(): String {

    delay(2000)

    return "New data"

}
```

withContext(Dispatchers.Main) ensures UI updates **run on the main thread**.

6. Handling Errors in Coroutines

Coroutines handle errors using **try-catch** and **exception handlers**.

Using Try-Catch in Coroutines

```kotlin
fun main() = runBlocking {

    launch {

        try {

            riskyTask()

        } catch (e: Exception) {

            println("Error: ${e.message}")

        }

    }

}

suspend fun riskyTask() {

    delay(1000)

    throw Exception("Something went wrong!")

}
```

Output:

Error: Something went wrong!

Prevents crashes by catching errors inside the coroutine.

Coroutines simplify asynchronous programming in Kotlin.

Suspend functions allow pausing execution without blocking.

Coroutine builders (launch**, **async**)** provide flexible execution.

Scopes and dispatchers ensure structured concurrency and efficient threading.

Error handling keeps coroutines safe from crashes.

Chapter 2: Android Development Fundamentals

Now that you're comfortable with Kotlin basics, it's time to delve into how Android apps are structured and how they function. In this chapter, we'll explore the anatomy of an Android project, get to know its core components like activities and fragments, learn how to design user interfaces, and understand how Android manages the lifecycle of its components. Let's dive in!

2.1 Understanding Android Project Structure

When you create a new Android project in **Android Studio**, you might feel overwhelmed by the number of files and folders. However, understanding the **Android project structure** is key to **efficient development, debugging, and maintenance**.

In this section we'll break down the structure of an **Android project**, explaining what each component does and how they work together to build your app.

1. Overview of Android Project Structure

A typical **Android project** consists of multiple directories and files, each serving a specific purpose.

Here's a **high-level view** of the **Android project structure** in Android Studio:

MyApp/

  ├── app/

  │ ├── src/

  │ │ ├── main/

```
|   |   |       ├── java/com/example/myapp/

|   |   |       ├── res/

|   |   |       ├── AndroidManifest.xml

|   |   ├── test/

|   |   ├── androidTest/

|   ├── build.gradle

├── build.gradle (Project-level)

├── settings.gradle
```

2. The app/ Module: The Heart of Your Project

The app/ directory is where most of your code and resources live. Inside app/, you'll find:

Directory/File	Purpose
src/main/	Contains your app's main source code and resources
src/test/	Unit tests for your app's logic

src/androidTest/	UI tests that run on real/emulated devices
build.gradle	Configuration file for the module (dependencies, settings)

3. src/main/ – The Core Development Folder

Inside src/main/, you'll find the following **three important parts**:

3.1 java/com/example/myapp/ (Kotlin/Java Code)

This is where your **Kotlin (or Java) source files** live.
 It contains:

  Activities and Fragments – UI controllers

  ViewModels – Manage UI-related data

  Repositories – Handle data fetching and storage

  Utilities and Helpers – Common functions

Example:

package com.example.myapp

import android.os.Bundle

import androidx.appcompat.app.AppCompatActivity

```
class MainActivity : AppCompatActivity() {

    override fun onCreate(savedInstanceState: Bundle?) {

        super.onCreate(savedInstanceState)

        setContentView(R.layout.activity_main)

    }

}
```

Tip: Organize code into packages (e.g., ui/, data/, network/) to keep it **maintainable**.

3.2 res/ (App Resources – Layouts, Images, Strings)

The res/ folder contains **resources** like XML layouts, images, strings, and more.

Subfolder	Purpose
layout/	XML files defining UI layouts
drawable/	Images, vectors, and UI elements
values/	Strings, colors, dimensions, and styles
mipmap/	App icons (for different screen sizes)

Example: A Simple Layout File (res/layout/activity_main.xml)

```xml
<?xml version="1.0" encoding="utf-8"?>

<LinearLayout xmlns:android="http://schemas.android.com/apk/res/android"

    android:layout_width="match_parent"

    android:layout_height="match_parent"

    android:orientation="vertical">

    <TextView

        android:id="@+id/textView"

        android:layout_width="wrap_content"

        android:layout_height="wrap_content"

        android:text="Hello, Kotlin!" />

</LinearLayout>
```

UI elements are defined in XML, then referenced in Kotlin code.

3.3 AndroidManifest.xml (App Configuration File)

The AndroidManifest.xml file is **essential** because it **declares app permissions, activities, and components**.

Example Manifest File

```xml
<manifest xmlns:android="http://schemas.android.com/apk/res/android"
```

```
package="com.example.myapp">

  <application

    android:allowBackup="true"

    android:theme="@style/Theme.MyApp">

      <activity android:name=".MainActivity">

        <intent-filter>

          <action android:name="android.intent.action.MAIN"/>

          <category android:name="android.intent.category.LAUNCHER"/>

        </intent-filter>

      </activity>

  </application>

</manifest>
```

The <activity> tag declares MainActivity as the **launch activity**.
The <intent-filter> ensures it **appears on the home screen**.

4. The gradle/ Folder: Build Configuration

Gradle is **Android's build system**, responsible for **compiling, linking, and packaging** your app.

There are **two Gradle files** you'll use frequently:

4.1 build.gradle (Module: app)

This **module-level Gradle file** defines dependencies and SDK versions.

Example:

```
android {

    compileSdkVersion 34


    defaultConfig {

        applicationId "com.example.myapp"

        minSdkVersion 21

        targetSdkVersion 34

    }

}

dependencies {

    implementation "androidx.core:core-ktx:1.12.0"
```

```
    implementation "androidx.appcompat:appcompat:1.6.1"

}
```

Defines **SDK versions, dependencies, and configurations** for the app.

4.2 build.gradle (Project Level)

This file manages **global settings**.

Example

```
buildscript {

    dependencies {

        classpath "com.android.tools.build:gradle:8.1.1"

    }

}
```

It ensures that Gradle knows **how to build Android projects**.

5. settings.gradle: Managing Project Modules

The settings.gradle file **registers all modules** in the project.

Example

```
include ':app'
```

It tells Gradle that the project contains an app module.

6. test/ and androidTest/: Writing Tests

Directory	Purpose
test/	Unit tests (Run on JVM)
androidTest/	UI and integration tests (Run on Android devices)

Example: Unit Test (test/)

```
import org.junit.Assert.assertEquals

import org.junit.Test


class ExampleUnitTest {

    @Test

    fun addition_isCorrect() {

        assertEquals(4, 2 + 2)

    }

}
```

Ensures functions work correctly **before integrating them into the app**.

By now, you should have a **clear understanding of the Android project structure**.

app/ contains **all your source code and resources**

res/ manages UI elements like layouts, images, and strings

AndroidManifest.xml configures your app's behavior

Gradle files (build.gradle, settings.gradle) handle **build settings and dependencies**

Test folders (test/, androidTest/) ensure your app is reliable

2.2 Activities, Fragments, and ViewModels

When building an Android app, understanding **Activities, Fragments, and ViewModels** is crucial. These components form the backbone of how an app **displays UI, manages navigation, and preserves data** across screen rotations and lifecycle events.

1. Understanding Activities

An **Activity** is a single, focused screen in an Android app. Every Android app must have at least **one** Activity, typically acting as the **entry point**.

Key Responsibilities of an Activity:

Handles **UI rendering**

Manages **user interactions**

Controls **navigation between screens**

Maintains the **lifecycle of the UI**

Creating a Simple Activity

When you create a new Android project in **Android Studio**, it automatically generates a **MainActivity** file. Here's a **basic Activity implementation**:

MainActivity.kt

package com.example.myapp

import android.os.Bundle

import androidx.appcompat.app.AppCompatActivity

class MainActivity : AppCompatActivity() {

    override fun onCreate(savedInstanceState: Bundle?) {

        super.onCreate(savedInstanceState)

        setContentView(R.layout.activity_main)

    }

}

Understanding the Code:

- onCreate(): Called when the Activity is first created.
- setContentView(R.layout.activity_main): Connects the Activity to an XML layout file (activity_main.xml).

Tip: Use **AppCompatActivity** instead of the default **Activity** class to access **modern Android features** (e.g., Jetpack components).

2. Fragments: Reusable UI Components

A **Fragment** represents a portion of UI within an Activity. It is a self-contained component that **can be reused across multiple Activities**.

Why Use Fragments?

Modular UI – Split UI into smaller, manageable parts

Reusability – Use the same Fragment in multiple Activities

Better tablet support – Adapt UIs based on screen sizes

Lifecycle awareness – Fragments work seamlessly with **ViewModels**

Creating a Simple Fragment

Let's create a HomeFragment that displays a **simple message**.

Step 1: Create HomeFragment.kt

```
package com.example.myapp

import android.os.Bundle

import android.view.LayoutInflater

import android.view.View

import android.view.ViewGroup

import androidx.fragment.app.Fragment
```

```kotlin
class HomeFragment : Fragment() {

    override fun onCreateView(

        inflater: LayoutInflater, container: ViewGroup?, savedInstanceState: Bundle?

    ): View? {

        return inflater.inflate(R.layout.fragment_home, container, false)

    }

}
```

Step 2: Define fragment_home.xml Layout

```xml
<?xml version="1.0" encoding="utf-8"?>

<LinearLayout xmlns:android="http://schemas.android.com/apk/res/android"

    android:layout_width="match_parent"

    android:layout_height="match_parent"

    android:orientation="vertical">

    <TextView

        android:id="@+id/textView"

        android:layout_width="wrap_content"

        android:layout_height="wrap_content"
```

```
        android:text="Welcome to Home Fragment!" />
```

```
</LinearLayout>
```

Step 3: Add Fragment to MainActivity.kt

To display the HomeFragment, we add it dynamically using FragmentManager.

```
supportFragmentManager.beginTransaction()

    .replace(R.id.fragment_container, HomeFragment())

    .commit()
```

Tip: Use replace() instead of add() to prevent multiple fragments from stacking up.

3. ViewModels: Managing UI Data Efficiently

A **ViewModel** stores and manages **UI-related data** in a **lifecycle-conscious** way. It **survives configuration changes**, such as **screen rotations**.

Why Use ViewModels?

Prevents UI data loss when the device rotates

Decouples UI from business logic

Works well with LiveData and Coroutines

Creating a Simple ViewModel

Step 1: Add ViewModel Dependency

```
dependencies {

    implementation "androidx.lifecycle:lifecycle-viewmodel-ktx:2.7.0"
```

}

Step 2: Create MainViewModel.kt

package com.example.myapp

import androidx.lifecycle.LiveData

import androidx.lifecycle.MutableLiveData

import androidx.lifecycle.ViewModel

```
class MainViewModel : ViewModel() {

    private val _message = MutableLiveData("Hello, ViewModel!")

    val message: LiveData<String> get() = _message

    fun updateMessage(newMessage: String) {

        _message.value = newMessage

    }

}
```

Step 3: Use ViewModel in MainActivity.kt

package com.example.myapp

import android.os.Bundle

import androidx.activity.viewModels

```kotlin
import androidx.appcompat.app.AppCompatActivity

import androidx.lifecycle.Observer

import kotlinx.android.synthetic.main.activity_main.*

class MainActivity : AppCompatActivity() {

    private val viewModel: MainViewModel by viewModels()

    override fun onCreate(savedInstanceState: Bundle?) {

        super.onCreate(savedInstanceState)

        setContentView(R.layout.activity_main)

        viewModel.message.observe(this, Observer { newText ->

            textView.text = newText

        })

    }

}
```

4. Bringing It All Together: Activity + Fragment + ViewModel

Now, let's **combine all three components**.

We will:

Create an **Activity** (MainActivity)

Use a **Fragment** (HomeFragment)

Store **data using a ViewModel** (HomeViewModel)

Step 1: Create HomeViewModel.kt

```kotlin
class HomeViewModel : ViewModel() {

    private val _text = MutableLiveData("Welcome to ViewModel!")

    val text: LiveData<String> get() = _text

}
```

Step 2: Update HomeFragment.kt

```kotlin
class HomeFragment : Fragment() {

    private val viewModel: HomeViewModel by viewModels()

    override fun onCreateView(

        inflater: LayoutInflater, container: ViewGroup?, savedInstanceState: Bundle?

    ): View? {

        val view = inflater.inflate(R.layout.fragment_home, container, false)

        val textView = view.findViewById<TextView>(R.id.textView)

        viewModel.text.observe(viewLifecycleOwner) { newText ->

            textView.text = newText

        }

        return view

    }
```

}

viewLifecycleOwner ensures **LiveData updates only while the Fragment is active**.

Next Steps:

- **Practice by creating multiple Fragments and switching between them**
- **Use ViewModel in real-world scenarios to handle LiveData and state management**
- **Experiment with Jetpack Navigation Component for better Fragment management**

2.3 UI Components and Layouts (XML vs Jetpack Compose)

Building a modern Android UI involves choosing between **XML-based layouts** (the traditional method) and **Jetpack Compose** (Google's new declarative UI framework).

1. The Traditional XML Approach

Android UI has historically been built using **XML (Extensible Markup Language)** to define layouts. These XML files are then linked to an **Activity or Fragment** where UI logic is handled.

Example: Creating a Simple XML Layout

Let's define a basic UI with **a TextView and a Button** in activity_main.xml:

activity_main.xml

```xml
<?xml version="1.0" encoding="utf-8"?>

<LinearLayout xmlns:android="http://schemas.android.com/apk/res/android"

    android:layout_width="match_parent"

    android:layout_height="match_parent"

    android:orientation="vertical"

    android:padding="16dp">

    <TextView

        android:id="@+id/textView"

        android:layout_width="wrap_content"

        android:layout_height="wrap_content"

        android:text="Hello, XML!"

        android:textSize="18sp" />

    <Button

        android:id="@+id/button"

        android:layout_width="wrap_content"

        android:layout_height="wrap_content"

        android:text="Click Me" />

</LinearLayout>
```

Handling UI Logic in Kotlin

In MainActivity.kt, we access these UI components using findViewById:

package com.example.myapp

import android.os.Bundle

import android.widget.Button

import android.widget.TextView

import androidx.appcompat.app.AppCompatActivity

class MainActivity : AppCompatActivity() {

  override fun onCreate(savedInstanceState: Bundle?) {

    super.onCreate(savedInstanceState)

    setContentView(R.layout.activity_main)

    val textView = findViewById<TextView>(R.id.textView)

    val button = findViewById<Button>(R.id.button)

    button.setOnClickListener {

      textView.text = "Button Clicked!"

    }

```
    }

}
```

Downside: findViewById() is verbose. Modern alternatives like **View Binding and Jetpack Compose** simplify UI interactions.

2. Jetpack Compose: The Modern UI Toolkit

Jetpack Compose is a **declarative UI framework** that eliminates XML entirely. Instead of defining layouts in XML, UI components are created directly in Kotlin code.

Why Use Jetpack Compose?

Simpler UI Code – No need for XML files

Reactivity Built-in – UI updates automatically when data changes

Better Performance – Optimized rendering

Easier Animation and Styling

Example: Creating the Same UI in Jetpack Compose

Step 1: Add Jetpack Compose Dependencies

In build.gradle (Module: app), enable Jetpack Compose:

```
android {

    composeOptions {

        kotlinCompilerExtensionVersion = "1.5.0"
```

```
        }

    }

dependencies {

    implementation "androidx.compose.ui:ui:1.6.0"

    implementation "androidx.compose.material3:material3:1.2.0"

    implementation "androidx.activity:activity-compose:1.8.0"

}
```

Step 2: Create the UI Using Compose

```
package com.example.myapp

import android.os.Bundle

import androidx.activity.ComponentActivity

import androidx.activity.compose.setContent

import androidx.compose.foundation.layout.*

import androidx.compose.material3.*

import androidx.compose.runtime.*

import androidx.compose.ui.Modifier

import androidx.compose.ui.unit.dp

class MainActivity : ComponentActivity() {
```

```kotlin
override fun onCreate(savedInstanceState: Bundle?) {

    super.onCreate(savedInstanceState)

    setContent {

        MyApp()

    }

}

}

@Composable

fun MyApp() {

    var text by remember { mutableStateOf("Hello, Jetpack Compose!") }

    Column(

        modifier = Modifier.padding(16.dp)

    ) {

        Text(text = text)

        Button(onClick = { text = "Button Clicked!" }) {

            Text("Click Me")

        }

    }
```

```
}
```

Breaking Down the Compose Code:

- setContent {} – Replaces setContentView(), rendering UI directly in Kotlin.
- @Composable – Marks a function as a **UI component**.
- mutableStateOf() – Enables **state management**.

Notice: There's **no need for XML, findViewById(), or even View Binding!**

3. Comparing XML vs Jetpack Compose

Feature	XML Layouts	Jetpack Compose
UI Definition	XML + Kotlin	Pure Kotlin
Reactivity	Requires LiveData/ViewModel	Built-in with State API
Code Complexity	More boilerplate (findViewById, View Binding)	Cleaner, concise code

| Animation Support | Requires XML + Kotlin | Simplified with Modifier API |
| Performance | Slightly slower (View system overhead) | More efficient rendering |

Verdict: While **XML is still valid**, **Jetpack Compose is the future** of Android UI development.

4. Advanced UI Components in Jetpack Compose

4.1 Lists & LazyColumn

Traditional RecyclerView can be replaced with LazyColumn:

```
@Composable

fun ItemList() {

    val items = listOf("Item 1", "Item 2", "Item 3")

    LazyColumn {

        items(items.size) { index ->

            Text(text = items[index], modifier = Modifier.padding(8.dp))

        }

    }
```

}

No need for **RecyclerView Adapter or ViewHolder**!

4.2 Navigation Between Screens

Jetpack Compose uses **Navigation Component**:

```
@Composable

fun NavigationExample(navController: NavController) {

    Column {

        Button(onClick = { navController.navigate("detail") }) {

            Text("Go to Detail Screen")

        }

    }

}
```

No need for **Intent or Fragment Transactions**.

5. Should You Switch to Jetpack Compose?

If you're starting a new project → Use **Jetpack Compose** for **simpler, faster development**.

If you're maintaining an existing project → Gradually migrate components **to Compose** while keeping XML for legacy parts.

Pro Tip: Google officially recommends Jetpack Compose as the **preferred way** to build Android UI.

Next Steps:

* **Try converting an existing XML layout to Jetpack Compose.**
* **Explore animations and custom components in Compose.**
* **Experiment with complex UI patterns like dynamic themes and state management.**

2.4 Handling User Input and Navigation

Handling user input and implementing seamless navigation are **core aspects of Android development**. Whether you're building a simple form or a multi-screen application, understanding how to capture user interactions and navigate between screens is essential.

1. Handling User Input

User input can come in many forms, such as **text input, button clicks, gestures, or touch events**. Let's explore how to handle them effectively.

1.1 Handling Text Input

The most common way to receive user input is through a **TextField (Jetpack Compose)** or **EditText (XML-based UI)**.

Example: XML-based EditText

```xml
<EditText

    android:id="@+id/editText"

    android:layout_width="match_parent"

    android:layout_height="wrap_content"

    android:hint="Enter text here" />
```

In your **Activity/Fragment**, capture the text input:

```kotlin
val editText = findViewById<EditText>(R.id.editText)

val userInput = editText.text.toString()
```

Issue: Requires findViewById(), which adds extra boilerplate.

Example: TextField in Jetpack Compose

```kotlin
@Composable

fun TextInputExample() {

    var text by remember { mutableStateOf("") }

    Column {

        TextField(

            value = text,

            onValueChange = { text = it },

            label = { Text("Enter text") }
```

```
    )

    Text("You typed: $text")

  }

}
```

Advantages of Compose: No need for findViewById(), state updates automatically.

1.2 Handling Button Clicks

XML Approach:

```
<Button

    android:id="@+id/button"

    android:layout_width="wrap_content"

    android:layout_height="wrap_content"

    android:text="Click Me" />
```

```
button.setOnClickListener {

    Toast.makeText(this, "Button Clicked!", Toast.LENGTH_SHORT).show()

}
```

Jetpack Compose Approach:

```
Button(onClick = { println("Button Clicked!") }) {

    Text("Click Me")

}
```

Compose is cleaner, with fewer lines of code.

1.3 Handling Gestures (Touch, Swipe, Drag & Drop)

Jetpack Compose simplifies gesture handling with **Modifier.pointerInput**.

Example: Detecting Tap Gestures

```
@Composable

fun GestureExample() {

    Box(

        modifier = Modifier

            .size(100.dp)

            .background(Color.Blue)

            .pointerInput(Unit) {

                detectTapGestures {

                    println("Box Tapped!")

                }
```

```
        }

    )

}
```

This replaces complex **OnTouchListener** implementations from XML-based UI.

2. Navigation in Android

Navigation lets users move between screens in an app. There are two main approaches:

1. **Explicit Intents (Traditional Approach)**
2. **Jetpack Navigation Component (Recommended)**

2.1 Traditional Navigation Using Intents

In older Android projects, navigation between activities is handled using **Intents**.

Example: Navigating from Screen A → Screen B

ScreenA.kt

```
val intent = Intent(this, ScreenB::class.java)

startActivity(intent)
```

ScreenB.kt

```
class ScreenB : AppCompatActivity() {
```

```
override fun onCreate(savedInstanceState: Bundle?) {

    super.onCreate(savedInstanceState)

    setContentView(R.layout.activity_screen_b)

}

}
```

Downsides:

Requires defining multiple activities.

Passing data between screens requires Intent.putExtra().

2.2 Jetpack Navigation Component (Recommended Approach)

Jetpack Navigation Component makes screen transitions easier by using a **NavController**.

Step 1: Add Dependencies

In build.gradle:

```
dependencies {

    implementation "androidx.navigation:navigation-compose:2.7.2"

}
```

Step 2: Define a Navigation Graph

```
@Composable

fun NavGraph(navController: NavHostController) {
```

```kotlin
NavHost(navController, startDestination = "screenA") {

    composable("screenA") { ScreenA(navController) }

    composable("screenB") { ScreenB() }

    }

}
```

Step 3: Navigate Between Screens

```kotlin
@Composable

fun ScreenA(navController: NavController) {

    Column {

        Text("Screen A")

        Button(onClick = { navController.navigate("screenB") }) {

            Text("Go to Screen B")

        }

    }

}
```

 No need for multiple activities—**Jetpack Compose uses one activity with multiple composable screens**.

3. Best Practices for User Input and Navigation

✔ **Use Jetpack Compose for Cleaner Code** – No findViewById(), better state management.

✔ **Ensure Accessibility** – Use contentDescription for buttons & images for **screen readers**.

✔ **Handle User Input Efficiently** – **Validate input** before submitting forms.

✔ **Optimize Navigation** – Avoid deep activity stacks; use **Navigation Component** for smooth transitions.

✔ **Manage Back Navigation Properly** – Always handle **Back Press Events** to prevent unwanted exits.

2.5 Lifecycle Management in Android

Managing an Android application's **lifecycle** is crucial for optimizing performance, preventing memory leaks, and ensuring a smooth user experience. Android apps go through different states, such as when an activity starts, stops, resumes, or is destroyed. Understanding how to handle these transitions effectively is key to writing reliable applications.

1. Understanding Android Lifecycle

An Android app does not run continuously; it goes through different states controlled by the **Android framework**. These states are defined by lifecycle methods in Activity and Fragment.

1.1 Activity Lifecycle

An Activity in Android goes through the following lifecycle stages:

1. **onCreate()** – Called when the activity is first created.

2. **onStart()** – The activity becomes visible to the user.

3. **onResume()** – The activity is now in the foreground and can interact with the user.

4. **onPause()** – The activity is still visible but is no longer in the foreground (e.g., a dialog appears).

5. **onStop()** – The activity is no longer visible to the user.

6. **onDestroy()** – The activity is being removed from memory.

Diagram: Activity Lifecycle

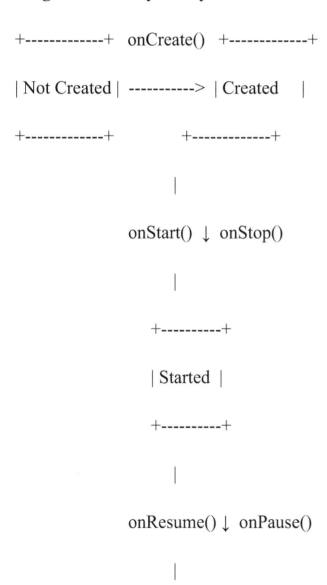

```
+-------------+  onCreate()  +-------------+

| Not Created | -----------> | Created     |

+-------------+              +-------------+

                                   |

                      onStart() ↓ onStop()

                                   |

                             +-----------+

                             | Started   |

                             +-----------+

                                   |

                      onResume() ↓ onPause()

                                   |
```

```
+---------+

| Resumed |

+---------+
```

Example: Overriding Lifecycle Methods in an Activity

```kotlin
class MainActivity : AppCompatActivity() {

    override fun onCreate(savedInstanceState: Bundle?) {

        super.onCreate(savedInstanceState)

        setContentView(R.layout.activity_main)

        Log.d("Lifecycle", "onCreate called")

    }

    override fun onStart() {

        super.onStart()

        Log.d("Lifecycle", "onStart called")

    }

    override fun onResume() {

        super.onResume()

        Log.d("Lifecycle", "onResume called")
```

```kotlin
    }

    override fun onPause() {

        super.onPause()

        Log.d("Lifecycle", "onPause called")

    }

    override fun onStop() {

        super.onStop()

        Log.d("Lifecycle", "onStop called")

    }

    override fun onDestroy() {

        super.onDestroy()

        Log.d("Lifecycle", "onDestroy called")

    }

}
```

 Why It's Useful: Helps track an activity's state for debugging or resource management.

1.2 Fragment Lifecycle

A Fragment is a reusable UI component inside an Activity. It has a **similar lifecycle** but with additional states:

1. **onAttach()** – The fragment is attached to an activity.
2. **onCreate()** – The fragment is created.
3. **onCreateView()** – The fragment creates its UI.
4. **onStart()** – The fragment becomes visible.
5. **onResume()** – The fragment is in the foreground.
6. **onPause()** – The fragment is partially visible.
7. **onStop()** – The fragment is no longer visible.
8. **onDestroyView()** – The fragment's UI is destroyed.
9. **onDestroy()** – The fragment is destroyed.
10. **onDetach()** – The fragment is detached from the activity.

Example: Fragment Lifecycle Methods

```
class MyFragment : Fragment() {

    override fun onCreate(savedInstanceState: Bundle?) {

        super.onCreate(savedInstanceState)

        Log.d("FragmentLifecycle", "onCreate called")

    }

    override fun onCreateView(inflater: LayoutInflater, container: ViewGroup?,
    savedInstanceState: Bundle?): View? {

        return inflater.inflate(R.layout.fragment_layout, container, false)

    }
```

```kotlin
override fun onResume() {

    super.onResume()

    Log.d("FragmentLifecycle", "onResume called")

}

override fun onDestroyView() {

    super.onDestroyView()

    Log.d("FragmentLifecycle", "onDestroyView called")

}

}
```

Key Difference: onCreateView() is specific to Fragments, while Activities use onCreate().

2. Handling Lifecycle Events in Modern Android

Instead of manually overriding lifecycle methods, Android provides **Lifecycle-aware components** to handle these changes efficiently.

2.1 Using LifecycleObserver

LifecycleObserver lets us perform actions based on lifecycle changes without modifying Activity code.

Example: Implementing a LifecycleObserver

```kotlin
class MyLifecycleObserver : DefaultLifecycleObserver {
```

```kotlin
    override fun onResume(owner: LifecycleOwner) {

        Log.d("LifecycleObserver", "App Resumed")

    }

    override fun onPause(owner: LifecycleOwner) {

        Log.d("LifecycleObserver", "App Paused")

    }

}
```

Attach it to an Activity or Fragment:

```kotlin
class MainActivity : AppCompatActivity() {

    override fun onCreate(savedInstanceState: Bundle?) {

        super.onCreate(savedInstanceState)

        lifecycle.addObserver(MyLifecycleObserver())

    }

}
```

 Advantage: Keeps the lifecycle logic separate from the Activity code.

2.2 Using ViewModel for Lifecycle-Aware Data Handling

A **ViewModel** survives configuration changes (e.g., screen rotations) and is independent of the Activity lifecycle.

Example: ViewModel Retains Data Across Config Changes

```
class MyViewModel : ViewModel() {

    val counter = MutableLiveData(0)

    fun incrementCounter() {

        counter.value = (counter.value ?: 0) + 1

    }

}
```

Use ViewModel in an Activity

```
class MainActivity : AppCompatActivity() {

    private val viewModel: MyViewModel by viewModels()

    override fun onCreate(savedInstanceState: Bundle?) {

        super.onCreate(savedInstanceState)

        setContentView(R.layout.activity_main)

        viewModel.counter.observe(this) { count ->

            textView.text = "Counter: $count"

        }

        button.setOnClickListener {

            viewModel.incrementCounter()
```

```
        }

    }

}
```

Why Use ViewModel?

✔ Prevents data loss when the screen rotates.

✔ Avoids memory leaks by keeping UI logic separate.

3. Best Practices for Lifecycle Management

Use ViewModel Instead of Storing Data in Activity

✔ Ensures **data persistence** across configuration changes.

Use LifecycleObservers Instead of Overriding Lifecycle Methods

✔ Reduces code in Activities/Fragments, improving maintainability.

Handle Background Tasks Properly (Using Coroutines)

✔ Use viewModelScope.launch {} inside ViewModel instead of running tasks in onCreate().

Release Resources in onDestroy() or onStop()

✔ Close database connections, unregister receivers, and clean up resources to prevent memory leaks.

Lifecycle management is a fundamental part of Android development. By leveraging **LifecycleObserver, ViewModel, and Jetpack libraries**, you can write efficient and maintainable code.

Next Steps:

- **Refactor your existing apps to use LifecycleObserver and ViewModel.**
- **Experiment with lifecycle-aware coroutines using** viewModelScope.
- **Explore advanced lifecycle topics like WorkManager for background tasks.**

By mastering Android's lifecycle management, you'll **write more resilient, efficient, and scalable Android apps!**

Chapter 3: Building Modern UI with Jetpack Compose

If you've ever built Android UIs using XML, you know how tedious and boilerplate-heavy it can be. Enter **Jetpack Compose**—a modern, declarative UI toolkit that makes designing Android interfaces as intuitive as writing Kotlin code.

In this chapter, we'll explore how to use Jetpack Compose to build beautiful, responsive UIs with less effort. You'll learn:

The basics of Jetpack Compose and how it differs from XML-based layouts.

How to create and customize UI components.

The importance of state management in Compose apps.

How to style and theme your app for a polished look.

Adding animations and transitions to enhance user experience.

3.1 Introduction to Jetpack Compose

Why Jetpack Compose?

For years, Android developers used XML-based layouts and imperative UI frameworks like AppCompat and ViewGroup. While these worked, they came with drawbacks:

Complex UI updates – Updating views required manually calling findViewById() and handling state changes.

Tightly coupled UI and logic – Managing UI state and business logic together often led to spaghetti code.

Performance issues – Deep view hierarchies slowed rendering.

Jetpack Compose, Android's modern **declarative UI toolkit**, solves these problems. Inspired by **React, SwiftUI, and Flutter**, Compose allows developers to **build UIs using composable functions, making UI development easier, faster, and more maintainable.**

What is Jetpack Compose?

Jetpack Compose is a **Kotlin-based UI toolkit** that follows a declarative programming model. Instead of **manipulating views directly**, developers **describe how the UI should look based on the current app state**, and Compose updates the UI automatically when the state changes.

Key Features:

✔ **Declarative UI** – No need to update views manually; UI updates when state changes.

✔ **Less Boilerplate** – No findViewById(), XML layouts, or Adapter classes.

✔ **Kotlin-First** – Fully written in Kotlin, simplifying code.

✔ **State-Driven UI** – UI automatically re-renders when data changes.

✔ **Interoperable** – Works with existing XML-based Views, making migration easier.

Getting Started with Jetpack Compose

1. Setting Up Jetpack Compose in an Android Project

Before writing your first Compose UI, ensure your Android project supports Jetpack Compose.

Step 1: Update build.gradle Files

Open your project's build.gradle (Module-level) and add:

```
android {

    compileSdk 34


    defaultConfig {

        minSdk 21

        targetSdk 34

    }


    buildFeatures {

        compose true

    }


    composeOptions {

        kotlinCompilerExtensionVersion '1.5.3'

    }

}
```

```
dependencies {

    implementation("androidx.compose.ui:ui:1.5.3")

    implementation("androidx.compose.material:material:1.5.3")

    implementation("androidx.compose.ui:ui-tooling-preview:1.5.3")

}
```

Step 2: Enable Jetpack Compose in Kotlin Compiler

Ensure kotlinOptions is set:

```
kotlinOptions {

    jvmTarget = "17"

}
```

2. Understanding Composable Functions

In Jetpack Compose, UI elements are defined using **functions annotated with @Composable**.

Basic Composable Function

```
@Composable

fun Greeting(name: String) {
```

```
    Text(text = "Hello, $name!")

}
```

✔ **No XML Needed** – The UI is fully defined in Kotlin.

✔ **Reusability** – The function can be used anywhere in your UI.

Calling a Composable from setContent()

In an Activity, use setContent {} to define the UI:

```
class MainActivity : ComponentActivity() {

    override fun onCreate(savedInstanceState: Bundle?) {

        super.onCreate(savedInstanceState)

        setContent {

            Greeting("Jetpack Compose")

        }

    }

}
```

3. Basic Layouts in Jetpack Compose

Compose provides **layout functions** like Column, Row, and Box to arrange UI elements.

Using Column, Row, and Box

```
@Composable

fun MyLayout() {

    Column(modifier = Modifier.fillMaxSize().padding(16.dp)) {

        Text(text = "Welcome to Jetpack Compose!", fontSize = 24.sp)

        Spacer(modifier = Modifier.height(10.dp))

        Button(onClick = { /* Do something */ }) {

            Text("Click Me")

        }

    }

}
```

✔ **Column** – Arranges elements vertically.

✔ **Row** – Arranges elements horizontally.

✔ **Box** – Overlaps elements on top of each other.

4. Styling and Theming in Jetpack Compose

Jetpack Compose supports theming via MaterialTheme.

```
@Composable

fun StyledText() {

    Text(
```

```kotlin
        text = "Styled Text",

        fontSize = 20.sp,

        fontWeight = FontWeight.Bold,

        color = Color.Blue

    )

}
```

You can also define a custom **theme** in Theme.kt:

```kotlin
@Composable

fun MyTheme(content: @Composable () -> Unit) {

    MaterialTheme(

        colorScheme = ColorScheme.light(

            primary = Color(0xFF6200EE),

            secondary = Color(0xFF03DAC5)

        ),

        typography = Typography(),

        content = content

    )

}
```

5. Handling State in Compose

Jetpack Compose uses remember and MutableState to manage UI state.

Example: Click Counter with State

```
@Composable

fun Counter() {

    var count by remember { mutableStateOf(0) }

    Column(horizontalAlignment = Alignment.CenterHorizontally) {

        Text(text = "Count: $count", fontSize = 24.sp)

        Button(onClick = { count++ }) {

            Text("Increase Count")

        }

    }

}
```

✔ **remember { mutableStateOf(0) }** – Stores state across recompositions.

✔ **Automatic UI Updates** – No need to manually refresh UI.

6. Previewing Jetpack Compose UIs

Compose allows **real-time previews** using @Preview.

```
@Preview(showBackground = true)

@Composable

fun PreviewGreeting() {

    Greeting("Android Developer")

}
```

✔ **Quick Iteration** – No need to recompile the app every time you make a UI change.

Jetpack Compose **revolutionizes UI development** in Android by making it declarative, state-driven, and less verbose.

 Jetpack Compose **replaces XML layouts** with **Kotlin functions**.
  Composable functions (@Composable) define UI elements.
  State management is easier with remember and mutableStateOf().
  MaterialTheme allows easy styling.
  Live previews speed up UI development.

Next Steps:

- ◆ Build a simple Compose UI with user interactions.
- ◆ Explore LazyColumn for lists and dynamic UI updates.
- ◆ Start migrating XML layouts to Compose in an existing project.

3.2 Creating UI Components in Compose

Jetpack Compose revolutionizes UI development by replacing XML-based layouts with **Composable functions**—self-contained building blocks that define your UI in Kotlin. These components are flexible, reusable, and easy to maintain. In this chapter, we'll explore how to create UI components in Compose and understand their role in modern Android development.

1. What Are UI Components in Jetpack Compose?

A **UI component** in Jetpack Compose is simply a function annotated with @Composable. These functions define UI elements, such as **buttons, text fields, images, and containers**, and can be nested to build complex interfaces.

Key Advantages of Compose UI Components:

 Reusable – Create once, use multiple times.
 Declarative – Define what the UI should look like, and Compose updates it automatically.
 Composable Functions – Build UI elements in a modular way.
 Customizable – Modify components with parameters like colors, padding, and alignment.

2. Creating Basic UI Components

Let's start with simple UI components: **Text, Button, Image, and Icon**.

Text Component

The Text composable is used to display text on the screen.

```kotlin
@Composable

fun GreetingMessage(name: String) {

    Text(

        text = "Hello, $name!",

        fontSize = 24.sp,

        fontWeight = FontWeight.Bold,

        color = Color.Blue

    )

}
```

Explanation:

✔ The text is dynamically set based on the name parameter.

✔ Styling is applied with fontSize, fontWeight, and color.

Button Component

Buttons trigger user interactions. Compose provides a Button composable.

```kotlin
@Composable

fun MyButton() {

    Button(onClick = { println("Button clicked!") }) {

        Text("Click Me")

    }
```

}

Explanation:

✔ onClick defines the action when the button is pressed.

✔ The button contains a Text component inside it.

Image Component

Images can be displayed using the Image composable.

@Composable

fun DisplayImage() {

    Image(

       painter = painterResource(id = R.drawable.my_image),

       contentDescription = "My Image",

       modifier = Modifier.size(100.dp)

)

}

Explanation:

✔ painterResource(id = R.drawable.my_image) loads an image from resources.

✔ contentDescription ensures accessibility.

✔ modifier.size(100.dp) sets the image size.

Icon Component

Icons can be displayed using the Icon composable.

@Composable

fun MyIcon() {

   Icon(

      imageVector = Icons.Default.Home,

      contentDescription = "Home Icon",

      tint = Color.Blue

)

}

Explanation:

✔ Uses Icons.Default.Home from Material Icons.

✔ tint sets the icon color.

3. Creating Custom UI Components

Now, let's create **custom reusable components** by combining multiple composables.

Example: A Custom Card Component

@Composable

fun UserProfileCard(name: String, imageRes: Int) {

```
Card(

    modifier = Modifier

        .fillMaxWidth()

        .padding(16.dp),

    elevation = 8.dp

) {

    Row(verticalAlignment = Alignment.CenterVertically) {

        Image(

            painter = painterResource(id = imageRes),

            contentDescription = "Profile Picture",

            modifier = Modifier

                .size(50.dp)

                .clip(CircleShape)

        )

        Spacer(modifier = Modifier.width(8.dp))

        Text(text = name, fontSize = 18.sp, fontWeight = FontWeight.Bold)

    }

}
```

}

Explanation:

✔ Uses Card to create an elevated surface.

✔ Arranges elements in a Row.

✔ Displays an image and text together.

✔ Uses clip(CircleShape) to create a circular profile picture.

4. Handling User Interaction in UI Components

Example: Custom Clickable Card

```
@Composable

fun ClickableCard(name: String, onClick: () -> Unit) {

    Card(

        modifier = Modifier

            .fillMaxWidth()

            .padding(16.dp)

            .clickable { onClick() },

        elevation = 8.dp

    ) {

        Text(

            text = name,
```

```
    fontSize = 20.sp,

    modifier = Modifier.padding(16.dp)

  )

  }

}
```

Explanation:

✔ clickable {} allows interaction.

✔ onClick is a lambda function passed from the caller.

5. Layout Components for UI Structure

Compose provides **layout components** to arrange UI elements:

Column (Vertical Layout)

```
@Composable

fun ColumnExample() {

  Column(

    modifier = Modifier.fillMaxSize(),

    horizontalAlignment = Alignment.CenterHorizontally

  ) {

    Text("First Item")
```

```
        Text("Second Item")

    }

}
```

✔ Elements are **stacked vertically**.

  ✔ horizontalAlignment = Alignment.CenterHorizontally centers the items.

Row (Horizontal Layout)

```
@Composable

fun RowExample() {

    Row(

        modifier = Modifier.fillMaxWidth(),

        horizontalArrangement = Arrangement.SpaceBetween

    ) {

        Text("Left")

        Text("Right")

    }

}
```

✔ Elements are **arranged horizontally**.

  ✔ Arrangement.SpaceBetween positions items at both ends.

Box (Overlay Layouts)

```
@Composable

fun BoxExample() {

    Box(

        modifier = Modifier.size(100.dp),

        contentAlignment = Alignment.Center

    ) {

        Text("Centered Text")

    }

}
```

✔ Box allows stacking UI elements.

✔ contentAlignment centers the child component.

6. Using Modifiers for Styling and Positioning

Modifiers in Compose **customize appearance, layout, and behavior**.

Common Modifiers:

```
@Composable

fun ModifierExample() {

    Text(

        text = "Styled Text",
```

```
modifier = Modifier

    .padding(16.dp)

    .background(Color.LightGray)

    .fillMaxWidth()

    .clickable { println("Clicked!") }

)

}
```

✔ padding(16.dp) – Adds spacing.

✔ background(Color.LightGray) – Sets background color.

✔ fillMaxWidth() – Makes the text expand.

✔ clickable {} – Adds interaction.

7. Previewing UI Components

Jetpack Compose allows live previews using @Preview.

```
@Preview(showBackground = true)

@Composable

fun PreviewUserProfile() {

    UserProfileCard(name = "John Doe", imageRes = R.drawable.profile_pic)

}
```

✔ **Instant UI previews** without running the app.

Compose UI components are **modular and reusable**.

Use **Text, Button, Image, and Icon** for basic UI.

Use **Column, Row, and Box** for structuring layouts.

Custom UI components help maintain **cleaner codebases**.

@Preview speeds up development.

Next Steps:

- Experiment with custom **composable functions**.
- Build a dynamic **list using LazyColumn**.
- Start migrating traditional XML layouts to Jetpack Compose.

With these tools, you can create **beautiful and efficient** Android apps using Jetpack Compose!

3.3 Managing State in Compose Applications

State management is one of the most important aspects of building modern Android applications. In Jetpack Compose, **state** determines what appears on the screen at any given time. Unlike the traditional View system, where UI elements are mutable and imperative, Compose follows a **declarative UI paradigm**, meaning the UI automatically re-renders when state changes.

1. Understanding State in Jetpack Compose

What is State?

State represents **data that can change** during the lifecycle of a UI component. When the state changes, the UI automatically re-composes itself to reflect the latest data.

Why is State Important?

✔ **Automatic UI updates** – No need to manually refresh the UI.

✔ **Predictable behavior** – Follows a clear data flow model.

✔ **Simplified code** – Less boilerplate compared to traditional Android UI updates.

Example of UI Without State (Static UI)

```
@Composable

fun Greeting() {

    Text("Hello, User!")

}
```

Problem: This text never changes because it lacks **state**.

2. Using MutableState in Compose

The mutableStateOf function allows you to create a state variable that triggers UI updates when changed.

Example: Using MutableState to Manage Text Input

@Composable

fun NameInput() {

  var name by remember { mutableStateOf("") }

  Column(modifier = Modifier.padding(16.dp)) {

    TextField(

      value = name,

      onValueChange = { name = it },

      label = { Text("Enter your name") }

)

    Text(text = "Hello, $name!")

  }

}

Explanation:

✔ mutableStateOf("") holds the name input.

✔ remember {} ensures state persists across recompositions.

✔ When the user types, the UI updates dynamically.

3. Remembering State with remember and rememberSaveable

State variables reset when the composable **restarts** (e.g., screen rotation).

Fixing State Reset with rememberSaveable

@Composable

fun Counter() {

    var count by rememberSaveable { mutableStateOf(0) }

    Column(modifier = Modifier.padding(16.dp)) {

        Text("Count: $count", fontSize = 20.sp)

        Button(onClick = { count++ }) {

            Text("Increase Count")

        }

    }

}

Key Difference:

✔ rememberSaveable retains state across configuration changes (like screen rotation).

✔ remember only retains state within a single recomposition.

4. Using State Hoisting for Better State Management

What is State Hoisting?

State hoisting is the practice of **lifting state** to a higher-level composable so that multiple components can access and modify it.

Example: Hoisting State to the Parent

```
@Composable

fun ParentScreen() {

    var username by rememberSaveable { mutableStateOf("") }

    Column {

        NameInputField(username) { username = it }

        GreetingMessage(username)

    }

}

@Composable

fun NameInputField(name: String, onNameChange: (String) -> Unit) {

    TextField(value = name, onValueChange = onNameChange, label = {
    Text("Enter Name") })

}

@Composable

fun GreetingMessage(name: String) {

    Text(text = "Welcome, $name!", fontSize = 20.sp)
```

}

Why Hoist State?

✔ Avoids unnecessary recompositions.

✔ Makes the UI easier to test and debug.

✔ Enables **separation of concerns**, making components reusable.

5. ViewModel for Complex State Management

For complex applications, **ViewModel** helps manage state beyond the composable lifecycle.

Example: Managing State with ViewModel

```kotlin
class CounterViewModel : ViewModel() {

    private val _count = mutableStateOf(0)

    val count: State<Int> = _count


    fun increment() {

        _count.value++

    }

}

@Composable

fun CounterScreen(viewModel: CounterViewModel = viewModel()) {
```

```
Column {

    Text("Count: ${viewModel.count.value}", fontSize = 20.sp)

    Button(onClick = { viewModel.increment() }) {

        Text("Increase Count")

    }

  }

}
```

Why Use ViewModel?

✔ **Persists state** across screen rotations.

✔ **Decouples UI logic** from the composables.

✔ **Handles complex business logic** efficiently.

6. Managing UI State with Kotlin Flow and LiveData

For **asynchronous** or **real-time data streams**, you can use **StateFlow, LiveData, or Flow**.

Example: StateFlow in ViewModel

```
class TimerViewModel : ViewModel() {

  private val _time = MutableStateFlow(0)

  val time: StateFlow<Int> = _time
```

```
init {

    viewModelScope.launch {

        while (true) {

            delay(1000L)

            _time.value++

        }

    }

}
```

Using StateFlow in a Composable

```
@Composable

fun TimerScreen(viewModel: TimerViewModel = viewModel()) {

    val time by viewModel.time.collectAsState()

    Text("Time: $time seconds")

}
```

Key Takeaways:

✔ StateFlow keeps state **reactive** and **efficient**.

✔ collectAsState() converts Flow into Compose-compatible state.

✔ Ideal for **live data updates** like timers, API polling, etc.

7. Best Practices for State Management in Compose

Use mutableStateOf **for simple UI updates.**

Use rememberSaveable **to persist state across rotations.**

Hoist state to the parent component when needed.

Use ViewModel **for non-UI state and complex logic.**

Use StateFlow **or** LiveData **for real-time data updates.**

Managing state effectively is **essential** for smooth, reactive, and bug-free UI development in Jetpack Compose. By using **remember, rememberSaveable, state hoisting, ViewModel, and Flow**, you can **build scalable and maintainable applications**.

Next Steps:

- Experiment with different state management techniques.
- Build an **interactive Compose UI** with multiple state-driven components.
- Explore **side effects in Compose**, such as LaunchedEffect and SideEffect.

With these tools, you're now equipped to manage state like a pro in Jetpack Compose.

3.4 Theming and Styling Your App

One of the biggest advantages of Jetpack Compose is its powerful and flexible **theming system**, which allows developers to create consistent and visually appealing UIs with ease. Whether you're building a **dark mode**, applying **custom typography**, or styling **buttons and cards**, Compose makes the process **declarative and reusable**.

In this chapter, we'll explore how to **customize themes, colors, typography, and shapes** in Jetpack Compose, with practical examples to help you style your app efficiently.

1. Understanding Theming in Jetpack Compose

In traditional Android development (XML-based UI), themes were defined using **styles.xml** and applied across activities and fragments. In Jetpack Compose, theming is much more flexible and dynamic.

Jetpack Compose themes are built using **MaterialTheme**, which consists of:

✔ **Colors** – Defines primary, secondary, and background colors.

✔ **Typography** – Defines font styles, sizes, and weights.

✔ **Shapes** – Defines the corner radius of UI components (e.g., buttons, cards).

Default Material Theme in Compose

By default, Jetpack Compose provides a Material theme wrapper:

```
@Composable

fun MyApp() {

  MyTheme {

    Surface(modifier = Modifier.fillMaxSize()) {

      Greeting("Android")

    }

  }
```

}

Here, MyTheme is a customizable theme that we'll define later.

2. Customizing Colors in Jetpack Compose

The ColorScheme class defines primary, secondary, background, and other colors. Let's create a **custom color palette**.

Defining Custom Colors

private val DarkColorScheme = darkColorScheme(

   primary = Color(0xFF1E88E5),

   secondary = Color(0xFF42A5F5),

   background = Color(0xFF121212),

   onPrimary = Color.White,

)

private val LightColorScheme = lightColorScheme(

   primary = Color(0xFF0D47A1),

   secondary = Color(0xFF1976D2),

   background = Color(0xFFFFFFFF),

   onPrimary = Color.Black,

)

Applying Colors in Your Theme

```
@Composable

fun MyTheme(content: @Composable () -> Unit) {

    val isDarkTheme = isSystemInDarkTheme()

    val colors = if (isDarkTheme) DarkColorScheme else LightColorScheme

    MaterialTheme(

        colorScheme = colors,

        typography = Typography,

        shapes = Shapes,

        content = content

    )

}
```

Key Takeaways:
- ✔ lightColorScheme and darkColorScheme define light and dark mode colors.
- ✔ isSystemInDarkTheme() automatically switches between modes.
- ✔ The MaterialTheme function applies colors globally.

3. Customizing Typography in Compose

Typography refers to **font sizes, weights, and styles** used across your app.

Defining Custom Typography

```
val CustomTypography = Typography(

    displayLarge = TextStyle(

        fontFamily = FontFamily.Serif,

        fontWeight = FontWeight.Bold,

        fontSize = 30.sp

    ),

    bodyLarge = TextStyle(

        fontFamily = FontFamily.SansSerif,

        fontWeight = FontWeight.Normal,

        fontSize = 16.sp

    )

)
```

Applying Typography in MaterialTheme

```
MaterialTheme(

    typography = CustomTypography

)
```

Using Custom Typography in Text Components

```
Text(
```

```
    text = "Welcome to Compose!",

    style = MaterialTheme.typography.displayLarge
```

)

Why Customize Typography?

✔ Enhances **readability** and **visual appeal**.

✔ Ensures **consistent text styles** across the app.

✔ Allows support for **custom fonts**.

4. Customizing Shapes in Jetpack Compose

Shapes define the **roundness of UI elements** like buttons, cards, and dialogs.

Creating a Custom Shape Scheme

```
val CustomShapes = Shapes(

    small = RoundedCornerShape(4.dp),

    medium = RoundedCornerShape(8.dp),

    large = RoundedCornerShape(16.dp)
```

)

Applying Shapes in MaterialTheme

```
MaterialTheme(

    shapes = CustomShapes
```

)

Using Shapes in Components

Card(

   shape = MaterialTheme.shapes.medium,

   modifier = Modifier.padding(16.dp),

   elevation = CardDefaults.cardElevation(defaultElevation = 4.dp)

) {

   Text("Styled Card", modifier = Modifier.padding(16.dp))

}

Why Customize Shapes?

✔ Creates a **unique visual identity**.

✔ Follows **Material Design guidelines**.

✔ Allows UI components to match **branding aesthetics**.

5. Implementing Dark Mode in Compose

Jetpack Compose makes it easy to **switch themes dynamically**.

Auto-Switching Between Light and Dark Mode

@Composable

fun MyApp() {

   val darkTheme = isSystemInDarkTheme()

```kotlin
val colors = if (darkTheme) DarkColorScheme else LightColorScheme

MaterialTheme(

    colorScheme = colors

) {

    // UI Content Here

}

}
```

Manually Switching Themes

```kotlin
@Composable

fun ThemeSwitcher() {

    var isDarkTheme by remember { mutableStateOf(false) }

    Column {

        Button(onClick = { isDarkTheme = !isDarkTheme }) {

            Text("Switch Theme")

        }

        MaterialTheme(
```

```
        colorScheme = if (isDarkTheme) DarkColorScheme else
LightColorScheme

    ) {

        Text("Theme Changed!", fontSize = 20.sp)

    }

  }

}
```

Dark Mode Benefits:

✔ **Battery Efficiency** – Saves power on OLED screens.

✔ **Eye Comfort** – Reduces strain in low-light conditions.

✔ **Modern Look** – Preferred by many users.

6. Best Practices for Theming in Compose

Keep themes modular – Define colors, typography, and shapes separately.

Use system settings – Implement isSystemInDarkTheme() for auto-dark mode.

Follow Material Design principles – Ensures UI consistency.

Reuse styles – Use MaterialTheme components for scalability.

Test themes on different devices – Ensures accessibility and visibility.

Theming and styling in Jetpack Compose is both **powerful and flexible**. By leveraging **MaterialTheme, ColorScheme, Typography, and Shapes**, you can create visually appealing and **consistent UI experiences**.

Next Steps:

- Experiment with **custom color palettes and typography**.
- Implement **light and dark mode switching** in your app.
- Explore **animations and motion** to enhance UI interactions.

3.5 Animations and Transitions in Compose

Animations add life to an app. Whether it's a subtle **fade-in effect**, a **smooth transition** between screens, or an engaging **button press animation**, they enhance user experience by making interactions feel **natural and responsive**.

Jetpack Compose makes animations easy with its **declarative API**, allowing you to create seamless UI effects **without complex XML-based animations**. In this Section,we'll explore different types of animations in Compose, how to implement them, and best practices for making your app feel polished.

1. Understanding Animations in Jetpack Compose

Jetpack Compose provides multiple ways to **animate UI elements**, including:

✔ animate*AsState – For animating values like size, color, or opacity.

✔ updateTransition – For handling **complex transitions** between UI states.

✔ AnimatedVisibility – For **showing and hiding** elements smoothly.

✔ rememberInfiniteTransition – For **looping animations** like pulsating effects.

✔ animateContentSize – For resizing components **dynamically**.

Let's explore each of these with practical examples.

2. Using animate*AsState for Simple Animations

If you need to animate **color, size, or opacity**, animate*AsState is the simplest approach.

Example: Animating a Button's Background Color

```
@Composable

fun ColorAnimationDemo() {

    var isClicked by remember { mutableStateOf(false) }

    val backgroundColor by animateColorAsState(

        targetValue = if (isClicked) Color.Red else Color.Blue,

        animationSpec = tween(durationMillis = 1000)

    )

    Button(

        onClick = { isClicked = !isClicked },

        colors = ButtonDefaults.buttonColors(containerColor = backgroundColor)

    ) {

        Text("Click Me")

    }

}
```

Key Takeaways:

✔ animateColorAsState animates between **two colors smoothly**.

✔ tween(durationMillis = 1000) controls the **animation speed**.

✔ Works well for **button presses, background changes, and status indicators**.

3. Animating Visibility with AnimatedVisibility

When elements **appear or disappear**, a sudden change looks unnatural. AnimatedVisibility helps create smooth transitions.

Example: Fading In and Out a Box

```
@Composable

fun VisibilityAnimationDemo() {

    var isVisible by remember { mutableStateOf(false) }

    Column {

        Button(onClick = { isVisible = !isVisible }) {

            Text(if (isVisible) "Hide Box" else "Show Box")

        }

        AnimatedVisibility(visible = isVisible) {

            Box(

                modifier = Modifier
```

```
            .size(100.dp)

            .background(Color.Green)

        )

    }

  }

}
```

Why Use AnimatedVisibility**?**

✔ Prevents UI elements from **popping in/out abruptly**.

✔ Supports multiple built-in animations like **fadeIn(), fadeOut(), scaleIn(), and scaleOut()**.

4. Using updateTransition **for Complex State Animations**

When animating **multiple properties simultaneously**, updateTransition is a better choice.

Example: Scaling and Rotating a Box Together

```
@Composable

fun TransitionAnimationDemo() {

  var isExpanded by remember { mutableStateOf(false) }

  val transition = updateTransition(targetState = isExpanded, label = "Box Animation")
```

```kotlin
val size by transition.animateDp(label = "Size Animation") { state ->

    if (state) 200.dp else 100.dp

}

val rotation by transition.animateFloat(label = "Rotation Animation") { state ->

    if (state) 360f else 0f

}

Column {

    Button(onClick = { isExpanded = !isExpanded }) {

        Text("Animate Box")

    }

    Box(

        modifier = Modifier

            .size(size)

            .graphicsLayer(rotationZ = rotation)

            .background(Color.Magenta)

    )

}
```

}

When to Use updateTransition**?**

✔ When animating **multiple properties at once** (e.g., size + rotation).

✔ When needing **better control over animations**.

5. Creating Infinite Animations with rememberInfiniteTransition

For **looping effects** like loading indicators, rememberInfiniteTransition is perfect.

Example: Pulsating Effect

```
@Composable

fun PulsatingEffect() {

    val infiniteTransition = rememberInfiniteTransition()

    val scale by infiniteTransition.animateFloat(

        initialValue = 1f,

        targetValue = 1.5f,

        animationSpec = infiniteRepeatable(

            animation = tween(1000),

            repeatMode = RepeatMode.Reverse

        )

    )
```

```
Box(

    modifier = Modifier

        .size(100.dp)

        .scale(scale)

        .background(Color.Cyan)

    )

}
```

Common Use Cases:

✔ **Pulsating buttons or icons**.

✔ **Indicating loading states** (e.g., animated dots).

6. Animating Layout Changes with animateContentSize

When UI elements **change size dynamically**, animateContentSize provides a **smooth expansion or collapse** effect.

Example: Expanding and Collapsing a Text View

```
@Composable

fun ExpandableText() {

    var expanded by remember { mutableStateOf(false) }
```

```
Column {

    Button(onClick = { expanded = !expanded }) {

        Text("Toggle Description")

    }

    Text(

        text = "This is an expandable text component that dynamically resizes
itself.",

        modifier = Modifier

            .animateContentSize()

            .background(Color.LightGray)

            .padding(16.dp),

        maxLines = if (expanded) Int.MAX_VALUE else 1

    )

}

}
```

Why Use animateContentSize?

✔ Ideal for **expanding/collapsing menus or text views**.

✔ Automatically **adjusts animation speed** based on content size.

7. Best Practices for Animations in Compose

Use animations sparingly – Avoid overloading UI with unnecessary animations.

Optimize performance – Keep animations smooth by testing on different devices.

Use remember for efficiency – Prevent recomposition from affecting animations.

Combine animations wisely – Mix updateTransition with animate*AsState for rich experiences.

Follow Material Design guidelines – Ensure animations feel natural and intuitive.

Animations in Jetpack Compose **enhance user experience** by making interactions smooth and engaging. Whether it's **fading elements in and out, pulsating buttons**, or **animating layout changes**, Compose provides **powerful tools** to create beautiful, fluid animations.

Next Steps:

* Experiment with AnimatedVisibility and animate*AsState.
* Try updateTransition for **complex UI animations**.
* Implement **dark mode transitions** for a polished effect.

Chapter 4: Data Management and Networking

In modern Android apps, data is everything. Whether you're storing user preferences, managing a local database, or fetching data from a remote API, how you handle data can make or break your app's performance and user experience.

4.1 Working with SharedPreferences and Room Database

In Android development, data persistence is essential. Whether you're saving a **user's theme preference**, **login state**, or **caching large datasets**, using the right storage mechanism is crucial.

1. Using SharedPreferences for Simple Data Storage

SharedPreferences is a lightweight API designed to store **primitive data types** (Boolean, Int, String, Float, etc.) as **key-value pairs**. It's best for:

✔ Storing **user settings** (e.g., dark mode, language preferences).
✔ Saving **authentication tokens**.
✔ Caching **simple app data**.

1.1 Writing Data to SharedPreferences

To store user preferences, use the SharedPreferences.Editor API.

Example: Saving a User's Theme Preference

```
class PreferenceManager(context: Context) {

    private val sharedPreferences = context.getSharedPreferences("AppPrefs",
Context.MODE_PRIVATE)
```

```
fun saveThemePreference(isDarkMode: Boolean) {

    sharedPreferences.edit().putBoolean("DARK_MODE", isDarkMode).apply()

}

fun getThemePreference(): Boolean {

    return sharedPreferences.getBoolean("DARK_MODE", false)

}

}
```

Key Takeaways:

✔ Context.MODE_PRIVATE ensures that data is **only accessible within the app**.

✔ .apply() saves changes **asynchronously** (use .commit() for synchronous saving).

✔ The data **persists across app launches**.

1.2 Reading Data from SharedPreferences

Retrieve the stored value by calling getBoolean(), getString(), etc.

Example: Applying the Theme Preference in MainActivity

```
class MainActivity : ComponentActivity() {

    private lateinit var prefs: PreferenceManager

    override fun onCreate(savedInstanceState: Bundle?) {
```

```
super.onCreate(savedInstanceState)

prefs = PreferenceManager(this)


val isDarkMode = prefs.getThemePreference()

val theme = if (isDarkMode) MaterialTheme.colorScheme.background else
Color.White


setContent {

    Box(modifier = Modifier.fillMaxSize().background(theme))

    }

  }

}
```

When to Use SharedPreferences?

✔ Ideal for **small, app-wide settings**.

✔ Avoid using it for **large datasets** or **structured data**.

2. Storing Complex Data with Room Database

For structured, **relational data**, Room is the preferred choice. It's an **SQLite wrapper** that simplifies database management using **Kotlin Coroutines and LiveData**.

2.1 Setting Up Room

Add the following dependencies to your build.gradle (Module) file:

```
dependencies {

    implementation "androidx.room:room-runtime:2.6.0"

    kapt "androidx.room:room-compiler:2.6.0"

    implementation "androidx.room:room-ktx:2.6.0"

}
```

Enable **Kotlin annotation processing** in gradle.properties:

```
kapt.incremental.apt=true
```

2.2 Defining a Room Entity (Data Model)

A **Room entity** represents a database table. Annotate a Kotlin data class with @Entity and define the primary key using @PrimaryKey.

Example: Defining a User Table

```
@Entity(tableName = "users")

data class User(

    @PrimaryKey(autoGenerate = true) val id: Int = 0,
```

val name: String,

val email: String

)

Key Points:

✔ @Entity(tableName = "users") creates a SQLite table.

✔ @PrimaryKey(autoGenerate = true) ensures unique IDs.

✔ Fields automatically map to **database columns**.

2.3 Creating a DAO (Data Access Object)

The DAO provides methods to **insert, update, delete, and query** database records.

Example: Creating a UserDao Interface

```
@Dao

interface UserDao {

    @Insert(onConflict = OnConflictStrategy.REPLACE)

    suspend fun insertUser(user: User)

    @Query("SELECT * FROM users")

    fun getAllUsers(): Flow<List<User>>

}
```

Why Use Flow<List<User>> **Instead of** List<User>?

✔ Flow enables **real-time updates** to the UI when the database changes.

✔ Room handles **database operations asynchronously** using coroutines.

2.4 Setting Up the Room Database

Create an **abstract class** that extends RoomDatabase.

Example: Creating AppDatabase

```
@Database(entities = [User::class], version = 1)

abstract class AppDatabase : RoomDatabase() {

    abstract fun userDao(): UserDao

    companion object {

        @Volatile

        private var INSTANCE: AppDatabase? = null

        fun getDatabase(context: Context): AppDatabase {

            return INSTANCE ?: synchronized(this) {

                val instance = Room.databaseBuilder(

                    context.applicationContext,

                    AppDatabase::class.java,

                    "app_database"

                ).build()
```

```
            INSTANCE = instance

            instance

        }

    }

  }

}
```

Key Takeaways:

✔ @Database(entities = [User::class], version = 1) defines **tables and schema version**.

✔ synchronized(this) ensures **singleton instantiation**.

✔ .databaseBuilder() creates a **persistent database**.

2.5 Performing Database Operations

To interact with Room, obtain a UserDao instance from AppDatabase.

Example: Inserting and Retrieving Users

```
class UserRepository(context: Context) {

  private val userDao = AppDatabase.getDatabase(context).userDao()

  suspend fun addUser(user: User) {

    userDao.insertUser(user)
```

```
}

fun getAllUsers(): Flow<List<User>> = userDao.getAllUsers()

}
```

2.6 Displaying Data in a Jetpack Compose UI

Use **StateFlow or LiveData** to observe Room data changes.

Example: Showing User List in Compose

```
@Composable

fun UserListScreen(viewModel: UserViewModel) {

    val users by viewModel.users.collectAsState(initial = emptyList())


    LazyColumn {

        items(users) { user ->

            Text("${user.name} - ${user.email}")

        }

    }

}
```

Best Practices for Room Integration in Compose:

✔ Use **ViewModel** + **StateFlow** for lifecycle-aware database updates.

✔ Avoid **blocking the UI thread** by using suspend functions.

✔ Prefer **Flow over List** for automatic UI updates.

3. When to Use SharedPreferences vs. Room Database?

Feature	SharedPreferences	Room Database
Data Type	Key-Value (Simple Data)	Structured (Relational Data)
Storage Size	Small	Large
Performance	Fast for small data	Optimized for large datasets
Querying Capabilities	No queries, only key-value	Supports SQL queries

Use Case	User settings, tokens	User data, cached API responses

4.2 Fetching Data from APIs Using Retrofit

In modern Android development, apps frequently need to fetch data from remote servers. Whether you're retrieving **weather updates, user profiles, or financial data**, making network requests efficiently is crucial.

1. Why Use Retrofit?

Retrofit is the **go-to HTTP client** for Android because:

✔ It **converts JSON into Kotlin objects** seamlessly.

✔ It supports **asynchronous execution** using coroutines.

✔ It has built-in support for **authentication and error handling**.

✔ It works **efficiently with Room Database and Jetpack Compose**.

Dependency:

Add this to your build.gradle (Module) file:

```
dependencies {

    implementation "com.squareup.retrofit2:retrofit:2.9.0"

    implementation "com.squareup.retrofit2:converter-gson:2.9.0"

    implementation "org.jetbrains.kotlinx:kotlinx-coroutines-android:1.6.4"
```

}

2. Setting Up Retrofit

To use Retrofit, we need:

1. **A data model (Kotlin class)** – Defines how the API response is structured.
2. **A Retrofit interface** – Defines API endpoints.
3. **A Retrofit instance** – Manages network requests.
4. **A ViewModel & UI layer** – Displays fetched data in Jetpack Compose.

3. Creating a Retrofit API Call

3.1 Define the Data Model

Assume we're fetching user data from an API like:

GET https://jsonplaceholder.typicode.com/users

Response:

```
[

  {

   "id": 1,

   "name": "John Doe",

   "email": "johndoe@example.com"

  }
```

]

Create a Kotlin **data class** to represent this response:

```kotlin
data class User(

    val id: Int,

    val name: String,

    val email: String

)
```

Why Use a Data Class?

✔ Converts API JSON into **Kotlin objects** automatically.

✔ Supports **immutability** and **easy serialization**.

3.2 Define API Endpoints with Retrofit Interface

Create an interface that **maps API endpoints**:

```kotlin
import retrofit2.http.GET

interface ApiService {

    @GET("users")

    suspend fun getUsers(): List<User>

}
```

Key Takeaways:

✔ @GET("users") makes a **GET request** to https://jsonplaceholder.typicode.com/users.

✔ The function returns List<User> thanks to **automatic JSON parsing**.

✔ suspend ensures that the function runs in **a coroutine** (non-blocking).

3.3 Build the Retrofit Instance

Now, set up Retrofit in a singleton object:

```
import retrofit2.Retrofit

import retrofit2.converter.gson.GsonConverterFactory


object RetrofitInstance {

    private const val BASE_URL = "https://jsonplaceholder.typicode.com/"

    val api: ApiService by lazy {

        Retrofit.Builder()

            .baseUrl(BASE_URL)

            .addConverterFactory(GsonConverterFactory.create())

            .build()

            .create(ApiService::class.java)

    }
```

}

Explanation:

✔ BASE_URL is the **root URL** for all API calls.

✔ .addConverterFactory(GsonConverterFactory.create()) **automatically converts JSON** to Kotlin objects.

✔ .build().create(ApiService::class.java) **creates an instance** of ApiService.

4. Fetching Data in a ViewModel

4.1 Create a Repository to Manage API Calls

It's good practice to use a **repository layer** to separate **network logic** from UI.

```
import kotlinx.coroutines.flow.Flow

import kotlinx.coroutines.flow.flow

class UserRepository {

    private val api = RetrofitInstance.api

    fun fetchUsers(): Flow<List<User>> = flow {

        val users = api.getUsers()

        emit(users) // Emit the API response as a Flow

    }

}
```

Why Use Flow?

✔ Enables **real-time updates** when data changes.

✔ Works **natively with Compose & coroutines**.

4.2 Implement ViewModel with LiveData & StateFlow

Create a UserViewModel to fetch data and expose it to the UI.

```kotlin
import androidx.lifecycle.ViewModel

import androidx.lifecycle.viewModelScope

import kotlinx.coroutines.flow.MutableStateFlow

import kotlinx.coroutines.flow.StateFlow

import kotlinx.coroutines.launch


class UserViewModel : ViewModel() {

    private val repository = UserRepository()

    private val _users = MutableStateFlow<List<User>>(emptyList())

    val users: StateFlow<List<User>> = _users

    init {

        fetchUsers()

    }

    private fun fetchUsers() {
```

```
viewModelScope.launch {

    repository.fetchUsers().collect { userList ->

        _users.value = userList

    }

  }

 }

}
```

Key Concepts:

✔ MutableStateFlow<List<User>> stores **API response**.

✔ viewModelScope.launch ensures the API request runs **asynchronously**.

✔ collect { userList -> ... } updates _users with new data.

5. Displaying Data in Jetpack Compose

Finally, let's show the API data in a **LazyColumn**.

```
@Composable

fun UserListScreen(viewModel: UserViewModel = UserViewModel()) {

  val users by viewModel.users.collectAsState()

  LazyColumn {

    items(users) { user ->
```

```kotlin
            UserItem(user)

        }

    }

}

@Composable

fun UserItem(user: User) {

    Column(modifier = Modifier.padding(16.dp)) {

        Text(text = "Name: ${user.name}", fontWeight = FontWeight.Bold)

        Text(text = "Email: ${user.email}")

        Divider()

    }

}
```

Key Takeaways:

✔ collectAsState() listens for **real-time API updates**.

✔ LazyColumn **efficiently lists API items**.

✔ UserItem() **displays each user's details**.

6. Handling API Errors Gracefully

Network failures **happen frequently**. Use try-catch to prevent crashes.

Modify fetchUsers() in UserRepository:

```kotlin
fun fetchUsers(): Flow<Result<List<User>>> = flow {

    try {

        val users = api.getUsers()

        emit(Result.success(users))

    } catch (e: Exception) {

        emit(Result.failure(e))

    }

}
```

Now, in ViewModel, handle errors:

```kotlin
private fun fetchUsers() {

    viewModelScope.launch {

        repository.fetchUsers().collect { result ->

            result.onSuccess { _users.value = it }

            result.onFailure { Log.e("API Error", it.message ?: "Unknown error") }

        }

    }

}
```

7. When to Use Retrofit?

Feature	Retrofit
Fetching APIs	Excellent
Authentication	Supports tokens, OAuth
Large Responses	Handles efficiently
Caching	Supports interceptors

Alternatives?

✔ Volley – Good for simple API calls but lacks **automatic JSON conversion**.

✔ OkHttp – More **low-level** than Retrofit but offers better **control**.

By integrating **Retrofit with Kotlin Coroutines**, we can build **fast, efficient, and scalable** network requests in Android.

- **Use Retrofit** for API calls.
- **Use Flow & ViewModel** to manage data efficiently.
- **Handle errors gracefully** to prevent crashes.

Now, you can **fetch, display, and manage API data** in Android apps **seamlessly**!

4.3 Using Kotlin Flow and LiveData for Data Streams

Real-time data handling is crucial for modern Android applications. Whether you're fetching API responses, monitoring user input, or tracking database updates, managing data streams efficiently can **improve performance and user experience**.

This section explores **Kotlin Flow and LiveData**, two powerful tools for handling reactive data streams in Android. By the end, you'll understand:

✔ The difference between **Flow and LiveData**

✔ How to use **Flow for asynchronous data streams**

✔ How to manage **LiveData in ViewModel**

✔ When to use **Flow vs. LiveData**

1. What Are Data Streams?

A **data stream** is a continuous flow of data that updates over time. Examples include:

✔ **API responses that change frequently** (e.g., live sports scores)

✔ **Database changes in Room** (e.g., new messages in a chat app)

✔ **User interactions** (e.g., tracking clicks or text input)

Traditional approaches like callbacks and RxJava work, but they **introduce complexity**. Kotlin Flow and LiveData simplify handling **real-time data** efficiently.

2. Flow vs. LiveData: Key Differences

Feature	Kotlin Flow	LiveData

Threading	Works with **coroutines**	Runs on **main thread**
Lifecycle Awareness	No built-in awareness	Lifecycle-aware
Backpressure Handling	Supports **cold/hot streams**	Doesn't support backpressure
API Support	Ideal for **networking & database**	Great for **UI updates**

When to Use What?

✔ Use **Flow** when working with **databases, networking, or background processing**.

✔ Use **LiveData** when dealing with **UI updates in Jetpack Compose or XML**.

3. Working with Kotlin Flow

Kotlin Flow is **a coroutine-based API** that handles asynchronous data streams.

3.1 Creating a Simple Flow

A **Flow** emits values one at a time. Let's create a simple example that emits numbers:

```
import kotlinx.coroutines.flow.Flow
```

```
import kotlinx.coroutines.flow.flow
```

```kotlin
fun getNumbers(): Flow<Int> = flow {

    for (i in 1..5) {

        emit(i) // Emits values 1 to 5

        kotlinx.coroutines.delay(1000) // Simulates a delay

    }

}
```

Key Concepts:

✔ flow {} creates a **cold stream**, meaning it only starts emitting when collected.

✔ emit(i) sends a new value.

✔ delay(1000) simulates **network delay or heavy computation**.

3.2 Collecting Data from Flow

A Flow **does nothing until collected**. Here's how to collect the numbers:

```kotlin
import kotlinx.coroutines.*

import kotlinx.coroutines.flow.collect

fun main() = runBlocking {

    getNumbers().collect { value ->

        println("Received: $value")

    }

}
```

✔ **collect {}** **triggers the flow** and consumes emitted values.

✔ Runs inside runBlocking {} for simplicity (normally, you'd use a coroutine).

3.3 Using Flow in ViewModel

To fetch user data from an API using **Flow in a ViewModel**:

import androidx.lifecycle.ViewModel

import kotlinx.coroutines.flow.MutableStateFlow

import kotlinx.coroutines.flow.StateFlow

import kotlinx.coroutines.launch

class UserViewModel : ViewModel() {

    private val _users = MutableStateFlow<List<String>>(emptyList())

    val users: StateFlow<List<String>> = _users

    init {

      fetchUsers()

    }

    private fun fetchUsers() {

      viewModelScope.launch {

        getUsersFromApi().collect { userList ->

```
        _users.value = userList

    }

  }

}

private fun getUsersFromApi(): Flow<List<String>> = flow {

    emit(listOf("John", "Sarah", "Emma")) // Simulating API response

  }

}
```

Key Takeaways:

✔ MutableStateFlow<List<String>> stores the list of users.

✔ collect {} fetches and updates _users.value.

✔ Works efficiently with **Jetpack Compose**.

4. Working with LiveData

LiveData is lifecycle-aware, meaning it **automatically stops observing** when the UI is not active, preventing memory leaks.

4.1 Creating and Observing LiveData

Here's how to create **LiveData in ViewModel**:

import androidx.lifecycle.LiveData

```kotlin
import androidx.lifecycle.MutableLiveData

import androidx.lifecycle.ViewModel

class LiveDataViewModel : ViewModel() {

    private val _message = MutableLiveData<String>("Hello, World!")

    val message: LiveData<String> = _message

    fun updateMessage(newMessage: String) {

        _message.value = newMessage

    }

}
```

Key Concepts:

✔ _message (MutableLiveData) stores **UI state**.

✔ message (LiveData) **exposes immutable data** to the UI.

✔ updateMessage() updates LiveData, triggering UI updates.

4.2 Using LiveData in a Jetpack Compose UI

Jetpack Compose supports **LiveData** using collectAsState():

```kotlin
@Composable

fun MessageScreen(viewModel: LiveDataViewModel = LiveDataViewModel()) {

    val message by viewModel.message.observeAsState("")

    Column {
```

```
        Text(text = message)

        Button(onClick = { viewModel.updateMessage("New Message!") }) {

            Text("Update")

        }

    }

}
```

Key Takeaways:

✔ observeAsState() **listens for LiveData changes** and updates UI automatically.

✔ **No need to manually cancel observers**—LiveData handles it!

5. Flow vs. LiveData: When to Use Each

Use Case	Flow	LiveData
Network Requests	Yes	No
Database Changes	Yes (Room)	Yes
UI State Management	No	Yes

Lifecycle Awareness	No	Yes

Rule of Thumb:

✔ Use **Flow** for API calls, **database queries**, and real-time data.

✔ Use **LiveData** for **UI components** like text fields, toggles, and buttons.

6. Combining Flow and LiveData

In some cases, you **convert Flow into LiveData**:

```
fun getLiveDataFromFlow(): LiveData<List<String>> {

    return flow {

        emit(listOf("Apple", "Banana", "Cherry"))

    }.asLiveData()

}
```

✔ **Best of both worlds**—use Flow's power with LiveData's lifecycle awareness.

7. Best Practices

- ◆ **Use Flow for heavy tasks** (networking, Room).
- ◆ **Use LiveData for UI updates** (Compose, XML).
- ◆ **Convert Flow to LiveData** if needed (asLiveData()).
- ◆ **Prefer StateFlow over LiveData in Compose**, as it's more efficient.

✔ **Kotlin Flow** handles asynchronous data streams efficiently.

✔ **LiveData** simplifies UI state management in XML & Compose.

✔ **Use both together** for a modern, reactive Android architecture.

Now you're ready to **build responsive, real-time Android apps** with **Flow & LiveData**!

4.4 Dependency Injection with Hilt

Modern Android apps often have multiple components that need to interact efficiently. Without proper management, dependencies can create **tight coupling, boilerplate code, and testing difficulties**.

This is where **Dependency Injection (DI)** comes in, and **Hilt** is Android's recommended DI framework.

1. What is Dependency Injection (DI)?

1.1 The Problem Without DI

Consider an app where a UserRepository fetches user data:

```
class UserRepository {

    fun getUserData(): String {

        return "User Data"

    }

}
```

Now, an UserViewModel depends on UserRepository:

```
class UserViewModel {

    private val repository = UserRepository() // Bad practice!

    fun fetchUser() = repository.getUserData()

}
```

What's wrong here?

✔ **Tight coupling** – The ViewModel is directly responsible for creating the repository.

✔ **Hard to test** – We cannot swap UserRepository with a mock for unit testing.

✔ **Difficult maintenance** – Changing dependencies requires modifying multiple files.

2. How Hilt Solves This Problem

Hilt automates dependency injection, ensuring:

✔ **Loose coupling** – Components depend on **abstractions, not implementations**.

✔ **Easy testing** – Dependencies can be **mocked or replaced**.

✔ **Scalability** – New dependencies can be added without modifying existing classes.

2.1 Setting Up Hilt in an Android Project

1 **Add Hilt dependencies to build.gradle (Module level):**

```
dependencies {

    implementation "com.google.dagger:hilt-android:2.50"
```

```
kapt "com.google.dagger:hilt-compiler:2.50"
```

}

2 **Enable Hilt in** build.gradle **(Project level):**

```
plugins {

    id 'kotlin-kapt'

    id 'dagger.hilt.android.plugin'

}
```

3 **Initialize Hilt in the Application Class**

```
@HiltAndroidApp

class MyApp : Application()
```

 Why this step?
 ✔ Hilt needs to be initialized at the **application level** to manage dependencies globally.

3. Injecting Dependencies Using Hilt

3.1 Injecting a Repository into ViewModel

Step 1: Create a Repository Interface & Implementation

```
interface UserRepository {

    fun getUserData(): String
```

```
}

class UserRepositoryImpl @Inject constructor() : UserRepository {

    override fun getUserData() = "User Data from Repository"

}
```

Why Use an Interface?

✔ Allows for **easy swapping** of implementations (useful in testing).

Step 2: Provide the Repository with Hilt

Hilt **cannot inject interfaces** directly, so we use @Module and @Provides:

```
@Module

@InstallIn(SingletonComponent::class)

object RepositoryModule {

    @Provides

    fun provideUserRepository(): UserRepository = UserRepositoryImpl()

}
```

Key Concepts:

✔ @Module – Defines where dependencies are provided.

✔ @Provides – Tells Hilt how to create UserRepository.

✔ @InstallIn(SingletonComponent::class) – Ensures the repository is available **globally**.

Step 3: Inject Repository into ViewModel

```kotlin
@HiltViewModel

class UserViewModel @Inject constructor(

    private val repository: UserRepository

) : ViewModel() {


    fun fetchUser() = repository.getUserData()

}
```

Key Concepts:

✔ @HiltViewModel – Enables **dependency injection in ViewModels**.

✔ @Inject – Hilt automatically provides the required UserRepository.

Step 4: Use ViewModel in a Jetpack Compose UI

```kotlin
@Composable

fun UserScreen(viewModel: UserViewModel = hiltViewModel()) {

    val userData = viewModel.fetchUser()

    Text(text = userData)

}
```

Why Use hiltViewModel()?

✔ Automatically provides **Hilt-managed ViewModels** to Composables.

4. Injecting Dependencies in Retrofit (API Calls)

4.1 Setting Up Retrofit with Hilt

[1] **Add Retrofit dependencies**

```
dependencies {

    implementation "com.squareup.retrofit2:retrofit:2.9.0"

    implementation "com.squareup.retrofit2:converter-gson:2.9.0"

}
```

[2] **Create an API Interface**

```
interface ApiService {

    @GET("users")

    suspend fun getUsers(): List<User>

}
```

[3] **Provide Retrofit instance using Hilt**

```
@Module

@InstallIn(SingletonComponent::class)

object NetworkModule {

    @Provides

    fun provideRetrofit(): Retrofit {
```

```
    return Retrofit.Builder()

        .baseUrl("https://api.example.com/")

        .addConverterFactory(GsonConverterFactory.create())

        .build()

    }

    @Provides

    fun provideApiService(retrofit: Retrofit): ApiService {

        return retrofit.create(ApiService::class.java)

    }

}
```

4 Inject Retrofit into Repository

```
class UserRepository @Inject constructor(private val apiService: ApiService) {

    suspend fun fetchUsers() = apiService.getUsers()

}
```

✔ Now, Hilt **automatically provides** Retrofit and ApiService whenever needed!

5. Best Practices for Using Hilt

✔ **Use** @Inject **in constructors** – Avoid unnecessary modules.

✔ **Use** @Singleton **for global dependencies** (e.g., Retrofit, Database).

✔ **Use** @HiltViewModel **for ViewModels** instead of ViewModelProvider.

✔ **Test ViewModels with** HiltAndroidRule for isolated dependency injection.

6. Testing Hilt Dependencies

Hilt simplifies unit testing by allowing **fake dependencies**.

@HiltAndroidTest

class UserViewModelTest {

@get:Rule

var hiltRule = HiltAndroidRule(this)

@Inject

lateinit var userRepository: UserRepository

@Before

fun setup() {

  hiltRule.inject()

}

@Test

```
fun testUserData() {

    assertEquals("User Data from Repository", userRepository.getUserData())

}

}
```

✔ **Hilt handles dependency injection in tests**, making them **reliable and modular**.

Chapter 5: Advanced Android Concepts

Modern Android development requires more than just UI design and API calls. To build robust and scalable applications, developers need to **handle background tasks efficiently, integrate cloud services, enforce security best practices, and optimize performance**.

5.1 Background Tasks with WorkManager and Coroutines

In modern Android development, **background tasks** play a crucial role in ensuring a smooth user experience. Whether it's **syncing data, downloading files, sending notifications, or processing images**, these tasks should not block the main thread to avoid **UI lag or app crashes**.

Two of the best tools for managing background tasks in Android are:

✔ **WorkManager** – Ideal for **deferrable, persistent background tasks**, such as periodic data syncing or scheduled jobs.

✔ **Coroutines** – Best suited for **lightweight, short-lived asynchronous tasks**, such as making API requests or performing database queries.

This section explores both approaches with practical, step-by-step implementations.

Understanding the Need for Background Processing

The Android framework provides strict **threading policies** to prevent **ANRs (Application Not Responding)**. By default, the **main thread** (UI thread) should handle only UI-related operations. Running heavy computations or network operations on the main thread can cause:

 Freezing UI elements
 Slow response times
 Crashes due to blocked execution

To avoid this, we offload heavy tasks to background threads using **WorkManager or Coroutines**.

Using WorkManager for Persistent Background Tasks

Why WorkManager?

✔ **Guaranteed execution** – even if the app restarts or the device reboots.
✔ **Suitable for scheduled and long-running tasks** – such as syncing data or uploading files.
✔ **Supports constraints** – such as running only on Wi-Fi or when charging.

Step 1: Adding WorkManager Dependency

To use WorkManager, first add the required dependency in build.gradle:

```
dependencies {

    implementation "androidx.work:work-runtime-ktx:2.9.0"

}
```

Step 2: Creating a Worker Class

A **Worker** is a class where the background task is executed.

```
class MyWorker(context: Context, params: WorkerParameters) : Worker(context, params) {

    override fun doWork(): Result {

        Log.d("WorkManager", "Background task running...")

        // Simulate a background task

        Thread.sleep(3000)

        return Result.success()

    }

}
```

✔ The doWork() function runs on a **background thread** by default.

✔ You can return Result.success(), Result.failure(), or Result.retry() based on the task's outcome.

Step 3: Scheduling a Work Request

To schedule this worker, we create a **WorkRequest** and enqueue it:

val workRequest = OneTimeWorkRequestBuilder<MyWorker>().build()

WorkManager.getInstance(context).enqueue(workRequest)

✔ This runs the task **once**. To run it **periodically**, use PeriodicWorkRequestBuilder:

val periodicWork = PeriodicWorkRequestBuilder<MyWorker>(15, TimeUnit.MINUTES).build()

WorkManager.getInstance(context).enqueue(periodicWork)

Key Takeaways
✔ **Use WorkManager for long-running, guaranteed background tasks**
✔ **Supports scheduled and periodic tasks**

Using Coroutines for Lightweight Async Tasks

Why Coroutines?

✔ **Best for lightweight, non-persistent tasks**

✔ **More efficient than traditional threads**

✔ **Seamlessly integrates with LiveData and ViewModel**

Step 1: Adding Coroutine Dependencies

Ensure you have the Kotlin Coroutine dependencies:

```
dependencies {

    implementation "org.jetbrains.kotlinx:kotlinx-coroutines-android:1.7.1"

}
```

Step 2: Running Background Tasks with Coroutines

Coroutines allow background tasks to run in **structured concurrency** using viewModelScope or CoroutineScope.

Example: Fetching data from an API using Coroutines in ViewModel:

```
class MyViewModel : ViewModel() {

    fun fetchData() {

        viewModelScope.launch(Dispatchers.IO) { // Runs on background thread

            val result = fetchDataFromNetwork()

            withContext(Dispatchers.Main) { // Switches back to UI thread

                updateUI(result)
```

```
        }

    }

  }

}
```

Explanation

✔ Dispatchers.IO – Runs the task on a background thread.

✔ withContext(Dispatchers.Main) – Switches back to the main thread to update UI.

Step 3: Using CoroutineWorker for WorkManager + Coroutines

WorkManager supports **CoroutineWorker**, which allows coroutines inside WorkManager.

```
class MyCoroutineWorker(context: Context, params: WorkerParameters) :
CoroutineWorker(context, params) {

  override suspend fun doWork(): Result {

    delay(2000) // Simulate work

    Log.d("CoroutineWorker", "Background task completed")

    return Result.success()

  }

}
```

To enqueue this worker:

```
val workRequest = OneTimeWorkRequestBuilder<MyCoroutineWorker>().build()
```

```
WorkManager.getInstance(context).enqueue(workRequest)
```

✔ **Combines the best of both worlds – structured concurrency of coroutines
with WorkManager's persistence.**

Comparing WorkManager and Coroutines

Feature	WorkManager	Coroutines
Use Case	Long-running tasks (sync, uploads)	Short-lived tasks (API calls, DB ops)
Persistence	Survives app restarts and device reboots	Runs only while the app is open
Scheduling	Supports periodic tasks	No built-in scheduling

| Threading | Runs on background thread automatically | Requires manual dispatchers |

When to Use What?

✔ Use WorkManager for **guaranteed execution** and **long-running tasks**.

✔ Use Coroutines for **lightweight, short-lived tasks** like fetching data.

✔ Use CoroutineWorker for **combining both approaches**.

✔ **WorkManager** is ideal for **persistent, scheduled tasks** like **data syncing or uploads**.

✔ **Coroutines** are perfect for **fast, short-lived async operations** like **API calls or database queries**.

✔ **CoroutineWorker** allows the best of **both WorkManager and Coroutines**.

Next Steps: Implement **WorkManager and Coroutines** in real-world scenarios to improve app performance!

5.2 Integrating Firebase: Authentication & Firestore

Firebase is a powerful **Backend-as-a-Service (BaaS)** that provides essential features like **authentication, real-time database, Firestore, cloud storage, and more**—without requiring a separate backend server. This makes it an excellent choice for modern **Kotlin Android apps** that need **scalability, real-time updates, and security**.

This section will cover **Firebase Authentication** (allowing users to sign in) and **Cloud Firestore** (storing user data in a scalable NoSQL database).

Why Use Firebase?

✔ **Easy to integrate** – No need to manage backend infrastructure.

✔ **Secure authentication** – Supports Google, Email/Password, Facebook, etc.

✔ **Scalable real-time database** – Firestore supports real-time syncing and offline mode.

✔ **Serverless backend** – Google manages scaling, reliability, and security.

1. Setting Up Firebase in an Android App

Before using Firebase services, we need to add Firebase to our project.

Step 1: Register Your App with Firebase

1. Visit **Firebase Console**.
2. Click **"Add project"**, name your project, and follow the setup instructions.
3. In the **Project Overview**, click **"Add App"** → **"Android"**.
4. Enter your **Android package name** (from AndroidManifest.xml).
5. Download the **google-services.json** file and place it in the app/ directory.

Step 2: Add Firebase Dependencies

Modify build.gradle (Project level) to include the Google services plugin:

```
buildscript {

  dependencies {

    classpath 'com.google.gms:google-services:4.4.0'

  }
```

}

Now, add the required dependencies in build.gradle (App level):

```
plugins {

    id 'com.google.gms.google-services'

}

dependencies {

    implementation 'com.google.firebase:firebase-auth-ktx:22.3.1' // Firebase
Authentication

    implementation 'com.google.firebase:firebase-firestore-ktx:24.10.0' // Firestore

}
```

Sync the project to apply the changes.

2. Implementing Firebase Authentication

Firebase Authentication allows users to sign in with **Email/Password, Google, Facebook, and more**.

Step 1: Enable Authentication Providers

1. In the **Firebase Console**, go to **Authentication** → **Sign-in method**.
2. Enable **Email/Password authentication**.

Step 2: Implement Email & Password Authentication

Sign Up New Users

Create an authentication instance:

val auth = FirebaseAuth.getInstance()

To **register a new user**, call:

```
fun signUpUser(email: String, password: String) {

  auth.createUserWithEmailAndPassword(email, password)

    .addOnCompleteListener { task ->

      if (task.isSuccessful) {

        Log.d("FirebaseAuth", "User registered: ${auth.currentUser?.uid}")

      } else {

        Log.e("FirebaseAuth", "Error: ${task.exception?.message}")

      }

    }

}
```

✔ If successful, Firebase automatically creates a new user and assigns a **unique UID**.

Login Existing Users

To **sign in an existing user**, use:

```
fun loginUser(email: String, password: String) {

    auth.signInWithEmailAndPassword(email, password)

        .addOnCompleteListener { task ->

            if (task.isSuccessful) {

                Log.d("FirebaseAuth", "User logged in: ${auth.currentUser?.uid}")

            } else {

                Log.e("FirebaseAuth", "Login failed: ${task.exception?.message}")

            }

        }

}
```

Logging Out Users

To log out the user:

```
auth.signOut()
```

Step 3: Display User Authentication State

To check if a user is logged in:

```
val user = auth.currentUser

if (user != null) {
```

```
    Log.d("FirebaseAuth", "Logged in as: ${user.email}")

} else {

    Log.d("FirebaseAuth", "No user logged in")

}
```

✔ **Next Step:** Store user data in Firestore.

3. Using Cloud Firestore to Store and Retrieve Data

Firestore is a cloud-based **NoSQL database** that stores data in **collections** and **documents**.

✔ **Collections** → Groups of related documents (e.g., users).
✔ **Documents** → Individual JSON-like objects (e.g., a user profile).

Step 1: Enable Firestore in Firebase Console

1. In **Firebase Console**, go to **Firestore Database**.
2. Click **Create Database** → **Start in Test Mode** (for development).
3. Click **Next** and complete the setup.

Step 2: Initialize Firestore

```
val db = FirebaseFirestore.getInstance()
```

Step 3: Writing Data to Firestore

To save **user profile data**, we create a users collection and add a document:

```kotlin
fun saveUserData(userId: String, name: String, age: Int) {

    val user = hashMapOf(

        "name" to name,

        "age" to age

    )

    db.collection("users").document(userId)

        .set(user)

        .addOnSuccessListener {

            Log.d("Firestore", "User data saved!")

        }

        .addOnFailureListener { e ->

            Log.e("Firestore", "Error saving data", e)

        }

}
```

✔ The document ID is set to the **user's UID**, ensuring each user has a unique document.

Step 4: Reading Data from Firestore

To retrieve and display user data:

```kotlin
fun getUserData(userId: String) {

    db.collection("users").document(userId).get()

        .addOnSuccessListener { document ->

            if (document.exists()) {

                val name = document.getString("name")

                val age = document.getLong("age")?.toInt()

                Log.d("Firestore", "User: $name, Age: $age")

            } else {

                Log.d("Firestore", "No such document")

            }

        }

        .addOnFailureListener { e ->

            Log.e("Firestore", "Error fetching data", e)

        }

}
```

✔ Firestore data is retrieved **asynchronously** to prevent UI freezing.

Step 5: Real-Time Updates with Firestore

Firestore allows **real-time listeners** that update UI automatically when data changes.

```kotlin
fun listenForUserUpdates(userId: String) {

  db.collection("users").document(userId)

    .addSnapshotListener { document, e ->

      if (e != null) {

        Log.e("Firestore", "Error listening for updates", e)

        return@addSnapshotListener

      }


      if (document != null && document.exists()) {

        val name = document.getString("name")

        val age = document.getLong("age")?.toInt()

        Log.d("Firestore", "Updated User: $name, Age: $age")

      }

    }

}
```

✔ **Live updates** are useful for chat apps, notifications, and collaborative apps.

Firebase Authentication simplifies user sign-in and identity management.

Firestore provides a **scalable, real-time, and secure** NoSQL database for storing app data.

Combining Authentication & Firestore allows us to create personalized user experiences.

Next Steps: Implement Firebase Authentication with Google Sign-In & explore Firestore Security Rules for better data protection!

5.3 Handling Permissions and Security Best Practices

Security is one of the most critical aspects of Android development. Poor security practices can lead to **data breaches, unauthorized access, and app vulnerabilities**. This chapter covers:

✔ **Android Permissions System** – How to request and handle permissions securely.

✔ **Best Security Practices** – Techniques to protect sensitive user data.

✔ **Common Security Pitfalls** – Mistakes to avoid when securing your app.

1. Understanding Android Permissions

Android permissions **control access to system resources** (camera, location, storage, etc.). Apps must request **only the permissions they truly need**.

Types of Permissions

Android categorizes permissions into three levels:

Type	Examples	Requires User Approval?
Normal Permissions	Internet, Bluetooth	No (automatically granted)
Dangerous Permissions	Camera, Location, Storage	Yes (explicit user consent)
Special Permissions	Draw over other apps, Install APKs	Yes (must be granted manually in Settings)

2. Requesting Permissions at Runtime

Since Android 6.0 (API 23+), apps must request **dangerous permissions** at runtime.

Step 1: Declare Permissions in AndroidManifest.xml

<uses-permission android:name="android.permission.CAMERA"/>

<uses-permission android:name="android.permission.ACCESS_FINE_LOCATION"/>

Step 2: Check and Request Permission at Runtime

Use **ContextCompat.checkSelfPermission** to check if permission is granted:

```kotlin
private fun checkCameraPermission(): Boolean {

    return ContextCompat.checkSelfPermission(

        this, Manifest.permission.CAMERA

    ) == PackageManager.PERMISSION_GRANTED

}
```

If permission is **not granted**, request it using ActivityCompat.requestPermissions:

```kotlin
private fun requestCameraPermission() {

    ActivityCompat.requestPermissions(

        this, arrayOf(Manifest.permission.CAMERA), REQUEST_CAMERA_CODE

    )

}
```

Handle user response in onRequestPermissionsResult:

```kotlin
override fun onRequestPermissionsResult(

    requestCode: Int, permissions: Array<out String>, grantResults: IntArray

) {

    super.onRequestPermissionsResult(requestCode, permissions, grantResults)
```

```
if (requestCode == REQUEST_CAMERA_CODE) {

    if (grantResults.isNotEmpty() && grantResults[0] ==
PackageManager.PERMISSION_GRANTED) {

        Log.d("Permissions", "Camera permission granted")

    } else {

        Log.e("Permissions", "Camera permission denied")

    }

}

}
```

✔ **Best Practice:** If the user denies permission **multiple times**, guide them to app settings:

```
Intent(Settings.ACTION_APPLICATION_DETAILS_SETTINGS,
Uri.parse("package:$packageName")).apply {

    startActivity(this)

}
```

3. Security Best Practices in Android Apps

1 Use Encrypted Storage for Sensitive Data

Never store sensitive data **in SharedPreferences or SQLite without encryption**. Instead, use:

- **Android EncryptedSharedPreferences**

```
val sharedPreferences = EncryptedSharedPreferences.create(

    "secure_prefs",

    MasterKeys.getOrCreate(MasterKeys.AES256_GCM_SPEC),

    applicationContext,

    EncryptedSharedPreferences.PrefKeyEncryptionScheme.AES256_SIV,

    EncryptedSharedPreferences.PrefValueEncryptionScheme.AES256_GCM

)

sharedPreferences.edit().putString("user_token", "secure_value").apply()
```

✔ **Why?** Data is encrypted before being stored, protecting against unauthorized access.

2 Avoid Hardcoding API Keys in the Code

Hardcoding API keys in source code is a major security risk. Instead:

- Use **Environment Variables** or **Firebase Remote Config**.
- Store secrets in a **.env file** (ignored in version control).
- For API keys in res/values, keep them in a **local properties file**:

```
def apiKey = project.hasProperty("API_KEY") ? project.property("API_KEY") :
""
```

✔ **Why?** API keys exposed in repositories can be misused by attackers.

3 Secure Network Communication with HTTPS & Certificate Pinning
Ensure all network calls use **HTTPS** with **TLS encryption** to prevent
Man-in-the-Middle (MITM) attacks.

```
<network-security-config>

  <domain-config cleartextTrafficPermitted="false">

    <domain includeSubdomains="true">your-secure-domain.com</domain>

  </domain-config>

</network-security-config>
```

✔ **Why?** This prevents attackers from intercepting sensitive user data over the network.

4 Implement User Authentication & Token Validation

- Use **Firebase Authentication or OAuth** for secure login.
- Store tokens **securely** using EncryptedSharedPreferences.
- Validate **JWT tokens** on the server before processing requests.

5 Restrict Permissions with the Least Privilege Principle

- **Do not request unnecessary permissions.**
- **Use foreground services** instead of requesting background location.
- **Avoid excessive storage access**—use scoped storage APIs instead.

6 Use ProGuard to Obfuscate Your Code

Obfuscation makes it harder for attackers to **reverse-engineer your app**.

Enable ProGuard by adding the following in proguard-rules.pro:

```
# Protect sensitive classes

-keep class com.example.app.utils.** { *; }
```

✔ **Why?** This prevents hackers from analyzing the APK and extracting sensitive logic.

7 Set Proper File & Database Permissions

- **Use MODE_PRIVATE** when storing files to restrict access.
- **Use Firestore Security Rules** to restrict unauthorized reads/writes:

```
rules_version = '2';

service cloud.firestore {

  match /databases/{database}/documents {

    match /users/{userId} {

      allow read, write: if request.auth.uid == userId;

    }

  }

}
```

✔ **Why?** This prevents unauthorized users from accessing other users' data.

Permissions should be requested **only when needed** to improve UX and security.

Secure Storage & Network Practices help prevent **data breaches**.

Following best security practices ensures your **app remains safe and compliant**.

Next Steps: Implement **Scoped Storage, Biometric Authentication, and Security Testing** for even greater protection!

5.4 Performance Optimization and Debugging

Optimizing app performance is essential to ensure smooth user experiences, reduce crashes, and improve battery life. Debugging, on the other hand, helps identify and resolve issues before they affect users.

1. Optimizing App Performance

1.1 Reducing Startup Time

Users expect apps to launch quickly. To speed up startup time:

Minimize the work done in Application class: Avoid heavy operations like database initialization in onCreate(). Use WorkManager or CoroutineScope.launch to defer tasks.

Enable ViewBinding instead of findViewById() for better performance.

Use Lazy Initialization to defer resource-intensive operations until needed:

val database: MyDatabase by lazy { MyDatabase.getInstance(context) }

Optimize Layout Hierarchy: Avoid deeply nested LinearLayouts. Use ConstraintLayout for better rendering efficiency.

Enable View Preloading:

Use android:placeholder **in Jetpack Compose to load lightweight placeholders before actual content.**

1.2 Improving Rendering Performance

Rendering lag occurs when UI operations take longer than 16ms per frame, causing janky animations and stutters.

Avoid Redundant Layout Draws: Use Profile GPU Rendering in Developer Options to detect slow frames.

Use RecyclerView Efficiently:

- **Use ViewHolder pattern to avoid inflating new views unnecessarily.**
- **Set setHasFixedSize(true) for static lists.**
- **Use DiffUtil instead of notifyDataSetChanged() for better performance.**

Reduce Overdraws:

Enable Show GPU Overdraw in Developer Options. Ideally, each pixel should be drawn only once.

Use Compose's remember to optimize recomposition
In Jetpack Compose, avoid unnecessary recompositions:

@Composable

fun OptimizedText(name: String) {

```kotlin
val greeting = remember { "Hello, $name!" }

    Text(greeting)

}
```

2. Managing Memory Efficiently

2.1 Preventing Memory Leaks

Memory leaks degrade app performance and can lead to OutOfMemoryErrors (OOMs).

Use Weak References in Singleton Classes
Singletons hold strong references that prevent garbage collection. Use WeakReference when necessary:

```kotlin
class Singleton private constructor(context: Context) {

    private val appContext = context.applicationContext

}
```

Close Database Cursors & Streams
Always close database cursors and input streams:

```kotlin
val cursor = db.rawQuery("SELECT * FROM users", null)

cursor?.use {
```

```
while (it.moveToNext()) {

    // Process data

  }

}
```

Avoid Anonymous Inner Classes

Use WeakReference to avoid memory leaks in long-lived objects:

```
class MyActivity : AppCompatActivity() {

    private val handler = Handler(Looper.getMainLooper())

    override fun onDestroy() {

        super.onDestroy()

        handler.removeCallbacksAndMessages(null) // Prevent leaks

    }

}
```

Use LeakCanary for Automatic Memory Leak Detection

Add the dependency in build.gradle:

```
dependencies {

    debugImplementation
"com.squareup.leakcanary:leakcanary-android:2.10"

}
```

3. Debugging Tools and Techniques

3.1 Using Android Studio Profiler

The Android Studio Profiler helps analyze CPU, memory, and network usage.

Steps to Use the Profiler:

1. Open Android Studio → View → Tool Windows → Profiler
2. Select CPU Profiler to detect slow functions.
3. Use Memory Profiler to check for memory leaks.
4. Analyze Network Profiler for slow API calls.

3.2 Logging and Debugging with Logcat

Logcat provides real-time debugging logs. Use different log levels to filter logs:

```
Log.d("DebugTag", "This is a debug message")
```

```
Log.e("ErrorTag", "An error occurred!", exception)
```

✔ Use conditional logging to avoid unnecessary logs in production:

```
if (BuildConfig.DEBUG) {

    Log.d("DebugTag", "Debug mode active")

}
```

3.3 Debugging Crashes with Firebase Crashlytics

Firebase Crashlytics provides real-time crash reporting.

Steps to Integrate Firebase Crashlytics:

1. Add Firebase Crashlytics dependency:

```
dependencies {

    implementation 'com.google.firebase:firebase-crashlytics-ktx:18.3.7'

}
```

2. Initialize Crashlytics in your app:

```
FirebaseCrashlytics.getInstance().setCrashlyticsCollectionEnabled(true)
```

3. Log non-fatal exceptions for better debugging insights:

```
try {

    // Some risky operation
```

```kotlin
} catch (e: Exception) {

    FirebaseCrashlytics.getInstance().recordException(e)

}
```

3.4 Analyzing Slow API Calls with OkHttp Logging

To debug slow network requests, enable logging with OkHttp Interceptor:

```kotlin
val loggingInterceptor = HttpLoggingInterceptor().apply {

    level = HttpLoggingInterceptor.Level.BODY

}

val client = OkHttpClient.Builder()

    .addInterceptor(loggingInterceptor)

    .build()
```

✔ Use Postman or Charles Proxy to analyze API request/response times.

Chapter 6: Testing and Deployment

Building an Android app is just the beginning. To ensure a smooth user experience, you need to **test, debug, optimize, and finally deploy** your app to the Play Store. In this chapter, we'll cover:

Writing **Unit and UI tests** with JUnit and Espresso

Debugging and profiling your app for **performance optimization**

Preparing and submitting your app to the **Google Play Store**

Monetization strategies like **ads, in-app purchases, and subscriptions**

By the end of this chapter, you'll be confident in **shipping a high-quality app that performs well and generates revenue**. Let's dive in!

6.1 Writing Unit and UI Tests (JUnit, Espresso)

Testing is a crucial step in Android development. It ensures that your app functions correctly, prevents regressions, and improves overall reliability.Here we will explore:

Unit testing with JUnit – Testing business logic and functions

UI testing with Espresso – Validating user interactions

Mocking dependencies – Using Mockito and Hilt for effective testing

1. Unit Testing with JUnit

Unit tests focus on testing small, isolated units of code, such as functions or classes, without relying on Android framework components.

1.1 Setting Up JUnit in Android

JUnit is included by default in new Android projects. To ensure you have the latest version, add the dependency in build.gradle:

```
dependencies {

    testImplementation 'junit:junit:4.13.2'

}
```

1.2 Writing a Basic Unit Test

Let's say we have a Calculator class with an add() function:

```
class Calculator {
```

```kotlin
fun add(a: Int, b: Int): Int {

    return a + b

}

}
```

A corresponding unit test using JUnit would look like this:

```kotlin
import org.junit.Assert.*

import org.junit.Test

class CalculatorTest {

    private val calculator = Calculator()


    @Test

    fun testAddition() {

        val result = calculator.add(5, 3)

        assertEquals(8, result)

    }

}
```

1.3 Using @Before and @After for Test Setup

JUnit allows setting up resources before and after tests:

```kotlin
import org.junit.Before

import org.junit.After

class ExampleTest {

    private lateinit var calculator: Calculator

    @Before

    fun setup() {

        calculator = Calculator()

    }

    @After

    fun teardown() {

        // Clean up if necessary

    }

    @Test

    fun testAddition() {

        assertEquals(10, calculator.add(7, 3))

    }
```

```
}
```

2. Mocking Dependencies with Mockito

Often, we need to test classes that depend on external components like databases or APIs. Instead of using real implementations, we can use **Mockito** to create mock objects.

2.1 Adding Mockito to Your Project

```
dependencies {

    testImplementation "org.mockito:mockito-core:4.8.0"

}
```

2.2 Mocking API Calls in Unit Tests

Consider a UserRepository that fetches data from an API:

```
class UserRepository(private val api: UserApi) {

    suspend fun getUser(): User {

        return api.fetchUser()

    }

}
```

We can mock UserApi in our tests using Mockito:

```
import org.mockito.Mockito.*
```

```kotlin
import kotlinx.coroutines.runBlocking

import org.junit.Test


class UserRepositoryTest {

    private val api = mock(UserApi::class.java)

    private val repository = UserRepository(api)

    @Test

    fun testUserFetch() = runBlocking {

        `when`(api.fetchUser()).thenReturn(User("John Doe"))


        val result = repository.getUser()

        assertEquals("John Doe", result.name)

    }

}
```

3. UI Testing with Espresso

Espresso is an Android testing framework designed for UI tests. It allows us to interact with UI elements, perform actions, and verify expected behaviors.

3.1 Adding Espresso to Your Project

Add the following dependencies to your build.gradle:

androidTestImplementation 'androidx.test.espresso:espresso-core:3.5.1'

androidTestImplementation 'androidx.test.ext:junit:1.1.5'

androidTestImplementation 'androidx.test:runner:1.5.2'

Enable **JUnit 4 test runner** in androidTest package:

```
@RunWith(AndroidJUnit4::class)

class ExampleUITest {

    @get:Rule

    val activityRule = ActivityScenarioRule(MainActivity::class.java)

}
```

3.2 Writing a Basic UI Test

Suppose we have a **Login screen** with a username field, password field, and login button. We want to test if entering a username and password updates the UI correctly.

XML Layout (activity_login.xml)

```
<EditText

    android:id="@+id/username"

    android:hint="Enter Username"/>

<EditText
```

android:id="@+id/password"

android:hint="Enter Password"/>

<Button

android:id="@+id/loginButton"

android:text="Login"/>

Espresso UI Test (LoginActivityTest.kt)

```kotlin
import androidx.test.espresso.Espresso.onView

import androidx.test.espresso.action.ViewActions.*

import androidx.test.espresso.matcher.ViewMatchers.*

import androidx.test.espresso.assertion.ViewAssertions.*

import org.junit.Rule

import org.junit.Test

class LoginActivityTest {

    @get:Rule

    val activityRule = ActivityScenarioRule(LoginActivity::class.java)

    @Test

    fun testLoginInput() {

        // Enter username
```

```
onView(withId(R.id.username))

    .perform(typeText("testuser"), closeSoftKeyboard())

// Enter password

onView(withId(R.id.password))

    .perform(typeText("password123"), closeSoftKeyboard())

// Click Login Button

onView(withId(R.id.loginButton)).perform(click())

// Verify UI update (assume successful login shows a welcome message)

onView(withText("Welcome testuser!"))

    .check(matches(isDisplayed()))

  }

}
```

3.3 Testing RecyclerView Items with Espresso

Testing RecyclerView scrolling and item clicks:

```
onView(withId(R.id.recyclerView))


.perform(RecyclerViewActions.scrollToPosition<RecyclerView.ViewHolder>(10))
```

onView(withId(R.id.recyclerView))

.perform(RecyclerViewActions.actionOnItemAtPosition<RecyclerView.ViewHold

er>(2, click()))

3.4 Handling Asynchronous UI with IdlingResource

Espresso requires the UI to be idle before interacting with elements. If testing asynchronous tasks (e.g., network requests), use **IdlingResource**:

IdlingRegistry.getInstance().register(myIdlingResource)

4. Running Tests in Android Studio

Run unit tests:

- Open CalculatorTest.kt
- Click **Run > Run 'testAddition'**

Run UI tests:

- Open LoginActivityTest.kt
- Click **Run > Run 'testLoginInput'**

Run all tests from Terminal:

./gradlew testDebugUnitTest

./gradlew connectedAndroidTest

Unit tests with JUnit ensure business logic correctness.

Mockito allows mocking dependencies for effective testing.

Espresso provides a powerful way to test UI interactions.

Next Steps: Integrate **CI/CD with GitHub Actions** to automate testing and improve code quality!

6.2 Debugging and Profiling Your App

Debugging and profiling are essential skills for any Android developer. A well-debugged app leads to better performance, fewer crashes, and a smoother user experience.

1. Debugging with Logcat

Logcat is the primary tool for monitoring logs and debugging runtime issues in Android apps. It displays system messages, stack traces, and custom logs.

1.1 Writing Custom Log Messages

Use the Log class to print debugging information:

import android.util.Log

Log.d("MainActivity", "App started successfully")

Log.e("MainActivity", "Error fetching data", exception)

Log Level	Purpose
Log.v (Verbose)	Detailed logs, useful for debugging everything

Log.d (Debug)	Logs useful for debugging purposes
Log.i (Info)	General app information
Log.w (Warning)	Potential issues that don't crash the app
Log.e (Error)	Errors that need immediate attention

1.2 Filtering Logs in Logcat

- Open **Logcat** in Android Studio
- Use the **search bar** to filter logs by tag (e.g., MainActivity)
- Use **log levels** to focus on warnings or errors

To **clear logs**, click the **trash icon** in Logcat.

2. Debugging with Breakpoints

Breakpoints allow you to pause execution and inspect variables at runtime.

2.1 Setting a Breakpoint

1. Open a Kotlin file in **Android Studio**
2. Click the **gutter (left of the line numbers)** to set a breakpoint
3. Run the app in **Debug mode** (Shift + F9)
4. When execution hits the breakpoint, the debugger window opens

2.2 Inspecting Variables

- Hover over variables to view their values
- Use the **Variables pane** to explore objects
- Modify values in real-time to test changes

3. Using Android Studio Profiler

Android Studio Profiler helps you analyze your app's **CPU, memory, network, and energy consumption**.

3.1 Opening Profiler

1. Open Android Studio
2. Click **View > Tool Windows > Profiler**
3. Select your device and run the profiler

3.2 CPU Profiler: Identifying Performance Bottlenecks

- Run your app and **select the CPU profiler**
- Choose **Sampling** (low overhead) or **Instrumented** (detailed) mode
- View function execution times and optimize slow operations

Example: Optimizing an inefficient loop

```
val list = List(100000) { it * 2 }

list.forEach {

    Log.d("Profiler", "Value: $it") // Bad: Causes Logcat spam
```

}

- ◆ **Solution:** Reduce logging and use efficient data structures.

3.3 Memory Profiler: Detecting Leaks

Memory leaks occur when objects are not properly released, leading to high RAM usage.

Common Causes of Memory Leaks:

- Retaining **Activity Context** in static variables
- Unregistered **BroadcastReceivers**
- Unreleased **listeners** or **callbacks**

Example of a Memory Leak:

object Singleton {

   var context: Context? = null // Bad practice

}

- ◆ **Solution:** Use WeakReference or ApplicationContext.

object Singleton {

   var context: WeakReference<Context>? = null

}

4. Network Debugging with Profiler & Stetho

4.1 Monitoring Network Requests in Profiler

- Open **Profiler > Network**
- Run your app and make API requests
- View **request URLs, response times, and data transfer sizes**

4.2 Debugging Network Requests with Stetho

Stetho is a debugging tool by Facebook that allows inspecting API calls via Chrome DevTools.

Adding Stetho to Your Project

Add the dependency:

```
dependencies {

    implementation 'com.facebook.stetho:stetho-okhttp3:1.6.0'

}
```

Initialize Stetho in Application class:

```
class MyApp : Application() {

    override fun onCreate() {

        super.onCreate()

        Stetho.initializeWithDefaults(this)

    }

}
```

Now, open **Chrome**, go to chrome://inspect, and inspect network calls in real-time!

5. Handling Crashes with Crashlytics

Use Firebase Crashlytics to collect and analyze crash reports.

5.1 Adding Crashlytics

1. Add the Firebase dependency:

```
dependencies {

    implementation 'com.google.firebase:firebase-crashlytics-ktx'

}
```

2. Initialize Crashlytics in your app:

```
FirebaseCrashlytics.getInstance().setCrashlyticsCollectionEnabled(true)
```

3. Force a crash for testing:

```
throw RuntimeException("Test Crash") // Will be logged in Firebase
```

View crashes in the **Firebase console** under **Crashlytics**.

Logcat is the first step for debugging runtime issues.

Breakpoints & Variable Inspection help analyze runtime behavior.

Android Studio Profiler detects CPU, memory, and network issues.

Crashlytics captures and analyzes crashes in production.

6.3 Preparing Your App for Google Play Store

Publishing your app on the **Google Play Store** is an exciting milestone. However, the process involves several critical steps, from configuring your app for release to complying with Google's policies. In this chapter, we'll cover:

Configuring your app for release

Generating a signed APK or AAB

Creating a Play Store developer account

Uploading your app and writing an optimized Play Store listing

Ensuring policy compliance and launching your app

1. Configuring Your App for Release

Before you publish your app, you need to **prepare your code for production** by:

- Removing debug logs (Log.d, Log.e, etc.)
- Switching from debug to release build configuration
- Optimizing resources (e.g., reducing image size, minifying code)

1.1 Updating AndroidManifest.xml

Ensure your manifest file is production-ready. Key considerations:

```
<manifest>

  <application

    android:allowBackup="false"  <!-- Prevents security issues -->

    android:usesCleartextTraffic="false"  <!-- Blocks non-HTTPS requests -->
```

android:networkSecurityConfig="@xml/network_security_config">

</application>

</manifest>

Pro Tip: Ensure you update the **version code and name** in build.gradle.

android {

   defaultConfig {

      versionCode 2

      versionName "1.1"

   }

}

2. Generating a Signed APK or AAB

Google Play requires either an **APK (Android Package Kit)** or **AAB (Android App Bundle)**. AAB is now the preferred format as it enables **dynamic delivery** and reduces app size.

2.1 Generating a Signed Build

1. Open **Android Studio**
2. Go to **Build > Generate Signed Bundle / APK**
3. Select **Android App Bundle (AAB)** or **APK**

4 Create or select a **Keystore**

5 Enter **Keystore credentials** (store this securely)

6 Click **Next > Finish**

Your signed **AAB** is now ready for Play Store upload.

3. Creating a Play Store Developer Account

To publish apps, you need a **Google Play Developer Account**:

1 Visit Google Play Console

2 Pay a **one-time** $25 registration fee

3 Complete your **developer profile**

4 Enable **Google Play App Signing** (recommended for security)

Once verified, you can publish apps under your **developer name**.

4. Uploading Your App to Google Play

Once logged into **Google Play Console**, follow these steps:

4.1 Creating a New App

1 Click **Create App**

2 Enter the **app name, default language, and category**

3 Choose **Free or Paid** (requires Merchant Account for paid apps)

4 Agree to **Google Play policies**

4.2 Uploading Your AAB/APK

- Navigate to **Release > Production > Create Release**
- Upload the **AAB or APK**
- Review and **enable Play App Signing**

5. Optimizing Your Play Store Listing

A well-optimized **Play Store listing** improves app discoverability.

5.1 Writing an Engaging App Description

- **First 2-3 lines** must **grab attention** (users rarely expand the full description)
- Highlight key **features and benefits**
- Use **relevant keywords** for better search rankings

Example:

Transform your productivity with **TaskMaster**!

Smart task reminders

AI-powered suggestions

Sync seamlessly across devices

5.2 Designing an Eye-Catching App Icon

Your **app icon** should be:

✔ Simple & recognizable

✔ High resolution (512×512 px)

✔ Consistent with your **brand identity**

Use Google's Material Design Guidelines for best results.

5.3 Uploading Screenshots & Promo Videos

Google Play allows up to **8 screenshots**. Key guidelines:

✔ Use **high-quality images** (1080px minimum)

✔ Show **real in-app screens**

✔ Add a **30-second promo video** (optional)

Use **Canva** or **Figma** for polished promotional graphics.

6. Ensuring Policy Compliance

Google Play enforces strict policies to maintain app quality and security.

6.1 Key Policies to Follow

✔ **Privacy Policy**: Required for all apps, hosted on a website

✔ **Permissions**: Request only necessary permissions

✔ **Content Guidelines**: No offensive or misleading content

✔ **Monetization Rules**: Follow Google Play's in-app purchase policies

Tip: Use Google Play's Policy Center to avoid violations.

7. Rolling Out & Publishing Your App

7.1 Testing with Internal, Closed, and Open Tracks

Before global launch, test your app with:

- **Internal testing** (trusted team members)
- **Closed beta** (select group of users)

- **Open beta** (public but limited release)

7.2 Launching Your App

1. **Submit for review** (Google takes ~24-48 hours)
2. After approval, click **Publish**
3. **Your app is live!**

AAB is the preferred format for Play Store apps

Optimize your Play Store listing with engaging text & images

Ensure Google policy compliance to avoid app removal

Test before launch to minimize post-release issues

Next Steps: Learn about **ASO (App Store Optimization)** to boost app downloads!

6.4 Monetization Strategies (Ads, In-App Purchases, Subscriptions)

Monetizing your Android app is a crucial step toward turning your development efforts into a sustainable revenue stream. Whether you want to offer a **free app with ads**, sell **premium features**, or build a **subscription-based business model**, Android provides multiple options for monetization.

In this section, we'll explore:

Advertising with Google AdMob

In-App Purchases (IAP) for premium features

Subscriptions for recurring revenue

Best practices to maximize earnings

1. Advertising with Google AdMob

Google AdMob allows you to display **ads** in your app and earn revenue based on **impressions and clicks**. Ads work well for free apps with large user bases.

1.1 Setting Up AdMob in Your App

1. **Sign up for Google AdMob** at https://admob.google.com/
2. Create an **ad unit** (banner, interstitial, rewarded, or native ads)
3. Integrate the **AdMob SDK** into your app

1.2 Adding a Banner Ad

First, add the **AdMob dependency** to your build.gradle:

```
dependencies {

    implementation 'com.google.android.gms:play-services-ads:22.5.0'

}
```

Initialize AdMob in your Application class:

```
class MyApp : Application() {

    override fun onCreate() {

        super.onCreate()

        MobileAds.initialize(this)

    }

}
```

Now, modify your activity_main.xml to display a **banner ad**:

```
<com.google.android.gms.ads.AdView

    android:id="@+id/adView"

    android:layout_width="match_parent"

    android:layout_height="wrap_content"

    ads:adSize="BANNER"

    ads:adUnitId="ca-app-pub-xxxxxxxxxxxxxxxx/xxxxxxxxx"/>
```

Finally, load the ad in your MainActivity.kt:

```
val adView: AdView = findViewById(R.id.adView)

val adRequest = AdRequest.Builder().build()

adView.loadAd(adRequest)
```

 Other Ad Types: You can also implement **Interstitial Ads** (full-screen), **Rewarded Ads** (user gets a reward), and **Native Ads** (customizable).

2. Implementing In-App Purchases (IAP)

In-App Purchases (IAP) allow users to buy **digital products, premium features, or consumable items** directly within your app.

2.1 Setting Up Google Play Billing

1 Add **Google Play Billing** dependency:

```
dependencies {

    implementation 'com.android.billingclient:billing:6.0.1'

}
```

2 Create **In-App Products** in the **Google Play Console**:

- Go to **Monetization > In-app products**
- Click **Create Product**
- Set a **unique product ID** (e.g., premium_upgrade)
- Set the **price** and **description**

2.2 Implementing IAP in Code

Initialize **BillingClient**:

```
val billingClient = BillingClient.newBuilder(this)

    .setListener { billingResult, purchases ->

        if (billingResult.responseCode == BillingClient.BillingResponseCode.OK
&& purchases != null) {

            for (purchase in purchases) {

                // Grant the purchased item to the user

            }
```

```kotlin
        }

    }

    .enablePendingPurchases()

    .build()
```

Query available products:

```kotlin
billingClient.startConnection(object : BillingClientStateListener {

    override fun onBillingSetupFinished(billingResult: BillingResult) {

        if (billingResult.responseCode == BillingClient.BillingResponseCode.OK) {

            val skuList = listOf("premium_upgrade")

            val params = SkuDetailsParams.newBuilder()

                .setSkusList(skuList)

                .setType(BillingClient.SkuType.INAPP)

                .build()

            billingClient.querySkuDetailsAsync(params) { billingResult,
skuDetailsList ->

                // Show purchase button if item is available

            }

        }
```

```
    }

    override fun onBillingServiceDisconnected() {}

})
```

Handle purchases:

```
fun handlePurchase(purchase: Purchase) {

    if (purchase.purchaseState == Purchase.PurchaseState.PURCHASED) {

        // Grant premium features to the user

    }

}
```

3. Implementing Subscriptions

Subscriptions allow users to pay **recurring fees** (monthly, yearly) for premium content.

3.1 Setting Up Subscriptions

1. Go to **Google Play Console > Monetization > Subscriptions**
2. Click **Create Subscription**
3. Set a **Product ID** (e.g., premium_monthly)
4. Choose **pricing** and **billing frequency**

3.2 Implementing Subscription in Code

The implementation is similar to In-App Purchases but uses
BillingClient.SkuType.SUBS.

```
val params = SkuDetailsParams.newBuilder()

    .setSkusList(listOf("premium_monthly"))

    .setType(BillingClient.SkuType.SUBS)

    .build()

billingClient.querySkuDetailsAsync(params) { billingResult, skuDetailsList ->

    if (billingResult.responseCode == BillingClient.BillingResponseCode.OK &&
skuDetailsList != null) {

        for (skuDetails in skuDetailsList) {

            val price = skuDetails.price

            // Show subscription UI

        }

    }

}
```

Handle **renewals and cancellations** using Play Billing's **purchase token**.

4. Best Practices for Monetization

4.1 Ads: Less is More

Don't overuse ads, as they can ruin user experience.

Use rewarded ads where users **choose** to watch for a benefit.

4.2 In-App Purchases: Focus on Value

✔ Offer **meaningful** upgrades (e.g., no ads, exclusive content)

✔ Provide **trial periods** for premium features

4.3 Subscriptions: Encourage Long-Term Users

✔ Offer **discounted annual plans**

✔ Provide **free trials** (7 days, 14 days)

4.4 Monitor Performance

Use **Google Play Console's revenue reports** to track performance

A/B test **pricing strategies**

Google AdMob is great for free apps with a large user base

In-App Purchases help sell premium features

Subscriptions generate **recurring revenue**

Use A/B testing to optimize your earnings

Next Steps: Implement **deep analytics** to understand user behavior and fine-tune your monetization strategy!

Chapter 7: Building a Complete App – A Hands-On Project

By now, you've learned the core concepts of **Kotlin and Android development**, from UI design to networking and data management. But theory alone isn't enough—you need to build something real!

In this chapter, we'll **develop a complete Android app from scratch**, applying everything you've learned so far.

Here's what we'll cover:

Planning the app structure – Defining features, choosing architecture

Implementing core features step by step – UI, data handling, APIs, navigation

Debugging and optimizing performance – Finding and fixing issues

Publishing and maintaining your app – Getting it on Google Play and keeping it updated

This will be an exciting, hands-on experience—let's build something awesome together

7.1 Planning the App Structure

Building a complete Android app from scratch requires careful planning. Without a clear structure, you may run into messy code, scalability issues, and maintenance headaches. In this section, we'll break down the essential steps to **design a well-structured Android application**, ensuring **clean architecture, modular components, and maintainability**.

1. Defining the App's Purpose and Features

Before writing code, define:

What problem does your app solve?
Who is your target audience?
What are the core features?

Example: If you're building a **task management app**, your core features might be:

- User authentication
- Task creation and management
- Notifications and reminders
- Cloud synchronization

Tip: Sketch a rough **user flow diagram** to visualize navigation between screens.

2. Choosing the Right Architecture

A well-structured app follows **separation of concerns**, making it easier to maintain. The recommended approach is the **MVVM (Model-View-ViewModel) architecture**, supported by **Jetpack libraries**.

2.1 MVVM Architecture Overview

Component	Responsibility	Example

Model	Manages data, interacts with API/database	TaskRepository
View	Displays UI, observes ViewModel	MainActivity.kt
ViewModel	Acts as a bridge between Model and View	TaskViewModel.kt

Why MVVM?

Separation of concerns → Avoids bloated Activity classes

Better testability → Easy to write unit tests

LiveData & Flow integration → Handles real-time updates efficiently

3. Structuring the Project Directory

A well-organized project improves scalability. Here's a **recommended directory structure**:

/app/src/main/java/com/example/taskmanager

```
|── data/          # Data sources (Room, Retrofit)
|   |── local/     # Local database (Room)
|   |── remote/    # API calls (Retrofit)
|   |── repository/  # Centralized data handling
```

```
|
|── domain/          # Business logic (Use Cases, Models)
|
|── ui/              # UI components (Activities, Fragments, Compose)
|   ├── main/        # Main screen
|   ├── tasks/       # Task list screen
|   ├── settings/    # Settings screen
|
|── viewmodel/       # ViewModels for each screen
|── di/              # Dependency Injection (Hilt)
|── utils/           # Helper functions & constants
|── navigation/      # Navigation management
```

Tip: Keeping **data, UI, and business logic separate** prevents code duplication and improves maintainability.

4. Choosing the Right Technologies

Your technology stack depends on your project requirements. Here's a recommended stack for a **modern Android app**:

Category	Recommended Library
UI Framework	**Jetpack Compose**
Navigation	**Jetpack Navigation Component**
State Management	**ViewModel + LiveData / Flow**
Database	**Room Database**
Network	**Retrofit + Kotlin Coroutines**
Dependency Injection	**Hilt**
Background Tasks	**WorkManager**

Testing   **JUnit, Espresso, MockK**

5. Planning App Screens and Navigation

5.1 Defining the Screens

For a **task management app**, we might have:

- ✔ **Splash Screen** – App logo, navigates to login/home
- ✔ **Login/Register Screen** – User authentication
- ✔ **Task List Screen** – Displays all tasks
- ✔ **Task Details Screen** – View/edit tasks
- ✔ **Settings Screen** – User preferences

5.2 Setting Up Jetpack Navigation

To manage navigation, use **Jetpack Navigation Component**:

1️⃣ Add dependency in build.gradle:

```
dependencies {

    implementation "androidx.navigation:navigation-compose:2.7.4"

}
```

2️⃣ Define a **NavHost** in MainActivity.kt:

```
@Composable
```

```kotlin
fun AppNavigation() {

    val navController = rememberNavController()

    NavHost(navController, startDestination = "taskList") {

        composable("taskList") { TaskListScreen(navController) }

        composable("taskDetails/{taskId}") { backStackEntry ->

            TaskDetailsScreen(taskId =
backStackEntry.arguments?.getString("taskId"))

        }

    }

}
```

3 Navigate between screens:

```kotlin
navController.navigate("taskDetails/${task.id}")
```

Tip: Keep navigation logic in a **separate file** to maintain clean code.

6. Managing State Efficiently

Using **ViewModel + StateFlow** ensures your UI updates reactively.

6.1 Creating a ViewModel

```kotlin
class TaskViewModel(private val repository: TaskRepository) : ViewModel() {

    private val _tasks = MutableStateFlow<List<Task>>(emptyList())
```

```kotlin
val tasks: StateFlow<List<Task>> = _tasks

fun fetchTasks() {

    viewModelScope.launch {

        _tasks.value = repository.getAllTasks()

    }

  }

}
```

6.2 Observing State in Compose UI

```kotlin
@Composable

fun TaskListScreen(viewModel: TaskViewModel) {

    val tasks by viewModel.tasks.collectAsState()

    LazyColumn {

        items(tasks) { task ->

            Text(task.title)

        }

    }

}
```

Why use StateFlow instead of LiveData?

- **Better performance**
- **More flexible** (works with coroutines)
- **No lifecycle dependency**

7. Designing a Scalable Backend (Optional)

If your app requires cloud data storage, consider:

Firebase Firestore – Real-time database with auto-sync

Supabase – Open-source alternative to Firebase

Backend with Kotlin Ktor – Build your own backend

Define **core features and user flow**

Follow **MVVM architecture** for maintainability

Organize files with **clean directory structure**

Use **Jetpack Compose + Navigation Component**

Manage **state with ViewModel + StateFlow**

Next Steps: Start implementing the core features, ensuring **clean, scalable, and maintainable code**!

7.2 Implementing Core Features Step by Step

Now that we've planned our app's structure, it's time to **bring it to life** by implementing its core features. In this section, we'll take a **step-by-step approach**, building essential functionalities with **Jetpack Compose, ViewModel, Room, and Retrofit**.

Our **example project** will be a **Task Management App**, where users can **add, edit, delete, and mark tasks as complete**.

1. Setting Up the Project

Before coding, ensure you have the necessary dependencies in your build.gradle file:

```
dependencies {

    // Jetpack Compose

    implementation "androidx.compose.ui:ui:1.5.1"

    implementation "androidx.lifecycle:lifecycle-viewmodel-compose:2.6.2"

    // Room Database

    implementation "androidx.room:room-runtime:2.5.2"

    kapt "androidx.room:room-compiler:2.5.2"

    // Retrofit for API Calls

    implementation "com.squareup.retrofit2:retrofit:2.9.0"

    implementation "com.squareup.retrofit2:converter-gson:2.9.0"

    // Coroutine support

    implementation "org.jetbrains.kotlinx:kotlinx-coroutines-android:1.6.4"

}
```

Once your project is set up, let's start **implementing features step by step**.

2. Implementing Local Storage with Room Database

2.1 Creating the Task Data Model

```
@Entity(tableName = "tasks")

data class Task(

    @PrimaryKey(autoGenerate = true) val id: Int = 0,

    val title: String,

    val description: String,

    val isCompleted: Boolean = false

)
```

2.2 Creating the DAO (Data Access Object)

```
@Dao

interface TaskDao {

    @Query("SELECT * FROM tasks ORDER BY id DESC")

    fun getAllTasks(): Flow<List<Task>>


    @Insert(onConflict = OnConflictStrategy.REPLACE)

    suspend fun insertTask(task: Task)
```

```kotlin
@Delete

suspend fun deleteTask(task: Task)


@Update

suspend fun updateTask(task: Task)

}
```

2.3 Setting Up the Room Database

```kotlin
@Database(entities = [Task::class], version = 1, exportSchema = false)

abstract class TaskDatabase : RoomDatabase() {

    abstract fun taskDao(): TaskDao

    companion object {

        @Volatile

        private var INSTANCE: TaskDatabase? = null


        fun getDatabase(context: Context): TaskDatabase {

            return INSTANCE ?: synchronized(this) {

                val instance = Room.databaseBuilder(
```

```kotlin
            context.applicationContext,

            TaskDatabase::class.java,

            "task_database"

        ).build()

        INSTANCE = instance

        instance

      }

    }

  }

}
```

3. Creating the Repository

The **repository** acts as an intermediary between the ViewModel and the data sources (Room & API).

```kotlin
class TaskRepository(private val taskDao: TaskDao) {

  val allTasks: Flow<List<Task>> = taskDao.getAllTasks()


  suspend fun insert(task: Task) {

    taskDao.insertTask(task)
```

```kotlin
    }

    suspend fun delete(task: Task) {

        taskDao.deleteTask(task)

    }

    suspend fun update(task: Task) {

        taskDao.updateTask(task)

    }

}
```

4. Creating the ViewModel

The **ViewModel** will expose the data and handle business logic.

```kotlin
class TaskViewModel(private val repository: TaskRepository) : ViewModel() {

    val tasks: StateFlow<List<Task>> = repository.allTasks.stateIn(

        scope = viewModelScope,

        started = SharingStarted.WhileSubscribed(5000),

        initialValue = emptyList()

    )

    fun addTask(task: Task) = viewModelScope.launch {

        repository.insert(task)
```

```
}

fun deleteTask(task: Task) = viewModelScope.launch {

    repository.delete(task)

}

fun updateTask(task: Task) = viewModelScope.launch {

    repository.update(task)

}

}
```

5. Building the UI with Jetpack Compose

5.1 Displaying a List of Tasks

```
@Composable

fun TaskListScreen(viewModel: TaskViewModel) {

    val tasks by viewModel.tasks.collectAsState()

    LazyColumn {

        items(tasks) { task ->

            TaskItem(task, onDelete = { viewModel.deleteTask(task) })

        }

    }
```

```
}
```

5.2 Creating a Task Item Component

```
@Composable

fun TaskItem(task: Task, onDelete: () -> Unit) {

    Row(

        modifier = Modifier

            .fillMaxWidth()

            .padding(8.dp)

            .background(Color.LightGray)

            .clickable { }

    ) {

        Column(modifier = Modifier.weight(1f)) {

            Text(text = task.title, fontWeight = FontWeight.Bold)

            Text(text = task.description)

        }

        IconButton(onClick = onDelete) {

            Icon(Icons.Default.Delete, contentDescription = "Delete Task")
```

```
      }

    }

}
```

5.3 Adding a New Task

```
@Composable

fun AddTaskScreen(viewModel: TaskViewModel, navController: NavController) {

    var title by remember { mutableStateOf("") }

    var description by remember { mutableStateOf("") }

    Column(modifier = Modifier.padding(16.dp)) {

        TextField(value = title, onValueChange = { title = it }, label = { Text("Title")
})

        TextField(value = description, onValueChange = { description = it }, label = {
Text("Description") })

        Button(onClick = {

            if (title.isNotBlank()) {

                viewModel.addTask(Task(title = title, description = description))

                navController.popBackStack()

            }

        }) {
```

```
        Text("Add Task")

    }

  }

}
```

6. Fetching Data from an API using Retrofit

To integrate external data, let's **fetch motivational quotes for tasks** using a free API.

6.1 Setting Up Retrofit

```
interface ApiService {

    @GET("random")

    suspend fun getQuote(): QuoteResponse

}

data class QuoteResponse(val content: String, val author: String)

object RetrofitInstance {

    private val retrofit = Retrofit.Builder()

        .baseUrl("https://api.quotable.io/")

        .addConverterFactory(GsonConverterFactory.create())

        .build()
```

```kotlin
    val api: ApiService = retrofit.create(ApiService::class.java)

}
```

6.2 Fetching and Displaying the Quote

```kotlin
class QuoteViewModel : ViewModel() {

    private val _quote = MutableStateFlow("")

    val quote: StateFlow<String> = _quote

    fun fetchQuote() {

        viewModelScope.launch {

            val response = RetrofitInstance.api.getQuote()

            _quote.value = "${response.content} - ${response.author}"

        }

    }

}

@Composable

fun QuoteScreen(viewModel: QuoteViewModel) {

    val quote by viewModel.quote.collectAsState()

    Column {
```

```
Text(quote, fontStyle = FontStyle.Italic)

Button(onClick = { viewModel.fetchQuote() }) {

    Text("Get a Quote")

  }

  }

}
```

We've **step-by-step implemented** the **core features** of a **Task Management App**:

 Set up **Room Database** for local storage

 Implemented **MVVM architecture** with **ViewModel & Repository**

 Built a **modern UI using Jetpack Compose**

 Integrated **Retrofit for fetching data from an API**

7.3 Debugging and Performance Optimization

Building a **Kotlin Android app** isn't just about writing code—it's about ensuring it runs **efficiently and smoothly**. Debugging and performance optimization are essential for creating an app that is **bug-free, responsive, and battery-efficient**.

In this section,we'll explore:

 Debugging techniques using Android Studio's built-in tools

 Performance profiling for UI, memory, and CPU

 Optimizations for faster rendering and lower battery consumption

1. Debugging Android Apps

1.1 Using Logcat for Debugging

Logcat is a built-in tool that shows real-time logs for your app. It's useful for **tracking errors, debugging crashes, and analyzing system events**.

Using Logcat in Kotlin

```kotlin
import android.util.Log

fun debugExample() {

    val userInput = "Hello, Android!"

    Log.d("DEBUG_TAG", "User Input: $userInput")

}
```

Log Levels:

- Log.d → Debug messages
- Log.e → Error messages
- Log.w → Warnings
- Log.i → Informational logs

 Tip: Use **filters** in Logcat (DEBUG_TAG) to find relevant logs faster.

1.2 Debugging with Breakpoints

Breakpoints allow you to **pause execution at a specific line** and inspect variables.

- **How to use breakpoints in Android Studio:**

1. Click in the **left margin** of your code editor to place a **red dot**.
2. Run your app in **Debug Mode (Shift + F9)**.

3. The execution will pause at the breakpoint—inspect variables in the **Debugger tab**.

Tip: Use **conditional breakpoints** (right-click on a breakpoint → Edit Condition) to pause execution only when a certain condition is met.

2. Performance Profiling and Optimization

A laggy app can frustrate users. Let's explore **profiling tools** to find performance bottlenecks.

2.1 Using Android Profiler

Open **Android Profiler** in Android Studio (**View → Tool Windows → Profiler**).

Key Profiling Tools:

CPU Profiler: Identifies slow functions

Memory Profiler: Tracks memory leaks

Network Profiler: Monitors API requests

Battery Profiler: Detects excessive power consumption

2.2 Reducing UI Lag (Jank) in Jetpack Compose

Jank (UI stuttering) happens when the UI takes too long to render.

Optimization Strategies:

Use LazyColumn for Lists: Avoid Column for long lists to improve scroll performance.

Bad Practice:

```
Column {

    items.forEach { item ->

        Text(text = item)

    }

}
```

Good Practice:

```
LazyColumn {

    items(items) { item ->

        Text(text = item)

    }

}
```

Avoid Recomposition with remember:

Jetpack Compose **recomposes UI** when data changes, but excessive recomposition is bad.

```
@Composable

fun OptimizedText(name: String) {

    val displayName = remember { name }

    Text(text = displayName)

}
```

2.3 Memory Leak Prevention

A **memory leak** happens when objects remain in memory even after they are no longer needed.

Common causes:

- Holding long-lived references to **Activity/Fragment**
- Using ViewModel incorrectly
- Not releasing listeners

Solution: Use WeakReferences or ApplicationContext

Bad Practice: Holding reference to Activity in a ViewModel

```
class MyViewModel(val context: Context) : ViewModel() { /* Leak-prone code */
}
```

Good Practice: Use applicationContext

```
class MyViewModel(application: Application) : AndroidViewModel(application) {
}
```

2.4 Optimizing API Calls with Retrofit

Slow API calls can freeze the UI. Use **Coroutines** for background execution.

```
class ApiRepository {
```

```kotlin
suspend fun fetchData(): List<Item> = withContext(Dispatchers.IO) {

    RetrofitInstance.api.getItems()

}

}
```

Enable Response Caching to reduce network usage:

```kotlin
val cacheSize = (5 * 1024 * 1024).toLong() // 5MB cache

val cache = Cache(context.cacheDir, cacheSize)

val okHttpClient = OkHttpClient.Builder()

    .cache(cache)

    .addInterceptor { chain ->

        var request = chain.request()

        request = request.newBuilder().header("Cache-Control", "public, max-age="
+ 60).build()

        chain.proceed(request)

    }

    .build()
```

2.5 Battery Optimization Best Practices

Apps that **overuse CPU, sensors, or wake-locks** drain battery quickly.

Reduce background work with WorkManager:

val workRequest = OneTimeWorkRequestBuilder<MyWorker>().build()

WorkManager.getInstance(context).enqueue(workRequest)

Use JobScheduler for periodic tasks
Avoid excessive wake locks

We explored **debugging techniques** (Logcat, breakpoints), **profiling tools** (CPU, memory), and **optimization strategies** (UI lag, API calls, battery life).

Next Steps: In the next section, we'll **prepare the app for publishing on the Google Play Store!**

7.4 Publishing and Maintaining Your App

Building an Android app is just the beginning. To make it accessible to users worldwide, you need to **publish** it on the Google Play Store. But launching an app isn't a one-time event—continuous **maintenance, updates, and user engagement** are crucial for long-term success.

In this section, we'll explore:

Preparing your app for release (signing, shrinking, and optimizing)
Publishing on the Google Play Store (step-by-step guide)
Maintaining and updating your app (user feedback, versioning)
Best practices for long-term success

1. Preparing Your App for Release

Before you can upload your app to the Play Store, you need to **optimize and secure** it.

1.1 Enabling ProGuard for Code Shrinking

Android apps contain **unused code, debugging symbols, and redundant resources**. **ProGuard (R8)** helps by:

Shrinking (removing unused code)

Obfuscating (making code harder to reverse-engineer)

Optimizing (improving runtime performance)

♦ **Enable ProGuard in** gradle.properties

android.enableR8=true

android.enableR8.fullMode=true

♦ **Configure ProGuard rules in** proguard-rules.pro

Keep essential classes

-keep class com.example.app.** { *; }

Remove logging statements

-assumenosideeffects class android.util.Log { *; }

Tip: Always test ProGuard configurations in **release mode** before publishing.

1.2 Generating a Signed APK or App Bundle

Google Play requires apps to be **signed** before release.

Steps to Generate a Signed Build in Android Studio:

1. **Go to** Build > Generate Signed Bundle/APK.
2. Select **Android App Bundle (AAB)** (recommended) or APK.
3. Create or select an **existing keystore**.
4. Set a **password and key alias** (keep it secure).
5. Select **release mode** and finish.

 Tip: AAB format is preferred because Google **optimizes** the app for different devices.

1.3 Preparing for Google Play Submission

Before uploading, ensure:

App version is updated (versionCode & versionName in build.gradle)

No unused permissions (check AndroidManifest.xml)

Privacy Policy is included (mandatory for apps that collect data)

Crash-free build (test using Firebase Crashlytics)

2. Publishing on the Google Play Store

2.1 Setting Up a Google Play Developer Account

To publish an app, you need a **Google Play Developer Account** ($25 one-time fee).

1. Go to **Google Play Console**

2. **Sign up** with your Google account

3. **Pay the registration fee**

4. **Complete account verification**

2.2 Creating a New App Listing

1. In **Google Play Console**, click **Create App**

2. Fill in:

   ○ **App Name**

   ○ **App Category** (e.g., Tools, Education)

   ○ **Privacy Policy URL**

2.3 Uploading the App Bundle (AAB)

1. Go to **"Production"** → **"Create Release"**

2. Upload your **signed AAB file**

3. **Set release notes** (explain what's new)

4. Click **Review & Rollout**

Tip: Use **internal testing** before full release to catch last-minute bugs.

2.4 Adding Store Listing Details

Users see your **app store listing** first. Optimize it for visibility.

Required Fields:

- **Title & Short Description** (catchy & keyword-rich)

- **Screenshots (5+ recommended)**

- **Feature Graphic (1024x500 px)**

- **App Icon (512x512 px, transparent background)**

- **Promo Video (optional but great for engagement)**

 Tip: Add keywords naturally in your description for **App Store Optimization (ASO)**.

3. Maintaining and Updating Your App

Once your app is live, your work isn't over. You need to **monitor, update, and optimize** for continued success.

3.1 Monitoring User Feedback and Crashes

 Check Play Console's "Reviews" tab for user feedback.

 Use Firebase Crashlytics to track crashes.

 Address negative reviews quickly to improve ratings.

```
FirebaseCrashlytics.getInstance().log("User experienced issue X")
```

3.2 Releasing App Updates

Every update needs:

 Updated version number (versionCode & versionName)

 Clear release notes (explain what's new)

 Beta testing before full rollout

 ◆ **Update build.gradle versioning before release:**

```
android {

  defaultConfig {
```

```
    versionCode 2

    versionName "1.1"


  }

}
```

3.3 Best Practices for Long-Term Success

Engage with Users → Respond to reviews and feedback.

Monitor Performance → Use Firebase, Google Analytics.

Keep the App Updated → Bug fixes, feature updates.

Optimize for New Android Versions → Stay ahead with new OS releases.

In this section, we covered **publishing and maintaining an Android app**—from **signing and uploading** to **monitoring and updating** for long-term success.

Next Steps: Now that your app is live, explore **monetization strategies** to generate revenue!

Conclusion and Next Steps

Congratulations! You've made it through this book and now have a **solid foundation in Kotlin Android development**. From setting up your environment to building and publishing a complete app, you've gained **hands-on experience** with modern tools and best practices.

But this is just the beginning. The world of **Android development is constantly evolving**, and there's always more to learn. In this final chapter, we'll discuss:

 Best practices to follow as a Kotlin Android developer

  Valuable resources to continue your learning journey

  Advanced topics like Kotlin Multiplatform and AI in mobile apps

Let's wrap things up and set you on the path to becoming a **pro Android developer**!

Best Practices for Kotlin Android Developers

To write **efficient, maintainable, and scalable** Android apps, follow these best practices:

1. Stick to the MVVM Architecture

Keeping UI logic separate from business logic makes your app **easier to manage and scale**.

Example: Use a ViewModel instead of handling logic inside an Activity.

class TaskViewModel(private val repository: TaskRepository) : ViewModel() {

    val tasks: LiveData<List<Task>> = repository.getTasks()

}

2. Use Jetpack Libraries

Google's Jetpack libraries provide **powerful tools** for Android development, such as:

Compose – For modern UI development

Room – For local database storage

Navigation Component – For handling screen transitions

WorkManager – For background tasks

Tip: Using Jetpack libraries ensures **long-term support** and compatibility with new Android versions.

3. Write Clean and Readable Code

Follow Kotlin's best practices for **clean, concise code**:

Use **extension functions** instead of utility classes

Prefer **sealed classes** over enums for state management

Use **coroutines and Flow** for async operations

Example: Using an extension function to format dates:

```
fun Long.toFormattedDate(): String {

    return SimpleDateFormat("dd MMM yyyy",
Locale.getDefault()).format(Date(this))

}
```

4. Optimize App Performance

A slow, laggy app drives users away. To optimize performance:

Use **LazyColumn** instead of RecyclerView for lists

Avoid **unnecessary recompositions** in Compose

Optimize database queries with **Room's indexing**

Minimize app size using **ProGuard and R8**

5. Test Your Code Regularly

Writing **unit and UI tests** prevents bugs and ensures smooth performance. Use:

JUnit for unit testing

Espresso for UI testing

MockK for mocking dependencies

Example: Testing a function in JUnit:

```
@Test

fun testAddition() {

    assertEquals(4, Calculator().add(2, 2))

}
```

Testing might feel like extra work, but it **saves time and effort in the long run**.

Resources for Further Learning

Android development is a journey, and staying updated is crucial. Here are some great resources to keep learning:

1. Official Documentation

Kotlin Documentation

Android Developers

Jetpack Compose

Tip: Always check the latest **Android API changes** to stay ahead.

2. Online Courses & Tutorials

JetBrains Academy

Udemy Android Kotlin Courses

Google's Android Developer Training

3. Community and Open Source Projects

Join developer communities to **learn from others and contribute**:

Reddit – r/androiddev

Stack Overflow – Ask and answer coding questions

GitHub – Explore open-source Android projects

4. YouTube Channels & Podcasts

- **Philipp Lackner** – Kotlin & Jetpack Compose tutorials
- **CodeWithChris** – Mobile development insights
- **Android Developers Podcast** – Latest trends and updates

Exploring Advanced Topics

Once you're comfortable with the basics, consider diving into **advanced Android development topics**.

- **1. Kotlin Multiplatform Mobile (KMM)**

KMM allows you to **share code between Android and iOS**, reducing development time for cross-platform apps.

How it works:

Write business logic in Kotlin

Share code across Android and iOS

Use platform-specific UI

Example: Shared Kotlin code for networking

```
expect fun fetchData(): String
```

```
actual fun fetchData(): String {

    return "Hello from Android!"

}
```

If you plan to build **cross-platform apps**, KMM is a great option!

2. AI and Machine Learning in Android

AI-powered apps are becoming the future! 🤖 You can integrate AI with:

ML Kit – Google's on-device ML library (Face detection, OCR, etc.)

TensorFlow Lite – Run deep learning models on Android

Chatbots – Use OpenAI or Google's Dialogflow for AI-driven interactions

Example: Using ML Kit for text recognition:

```
val recognizer =
TextRecognition.getClient(TextRecognizerOptions.DEFAULT_OPTIONS)

val result = recognizer.process(image)

    .addOnSuccessListener { text -> Log.d("ML", text.text) }
```

AI-powered apps **enhance user experience and engagement**.

3. Jetpack Compose Advanced Topics

Once you master the basics, try:

Custom UI components

Advanced animations

Compose performance optimizations

Example: Creating a smooth fade-in animation:

```
val alpha by animateFloatAsState(targetValue = 1f)

Box(modifier = Modifier.alpha(alpha)) {

    Text("Hello Compose!")
```

```
}
```

Jetpack Compose is the **future of Android UI**, so mastering it will keep you ahead of the curve.

Final Words – Keep Building!

You've come a long way, and now **you're ready to build real-world Android apps**!

Here's your next step:

Choose a personal project and start coding

Join developer communities and contribute to open-source projects

Keep learning and stay updated with new Android developments

Android development is an exciting journey—embrace the challenges, experiment with new ideas, and most importantly, **enjoy the process**!

This is not the end—it's just the beginning of your **Android developer journey**.

What's next?

I encourage you to **keep coding, experimenting, and sharing your knowledge**. Maybe one day, you'll be writing your own Android development book.

www.ingramcontent.com/pod-product-compliance
Lightning Source LLC
LaVergne TN
LVHW060121070326
832902LV00019B/3066